Companion to the

Africana Worship Book

Companion to the

Africana Worship Book

General Editors:
Valerie Bridgeman Davis, PhD
Associate Editor, Safiyah Fosua

DISCIPLESHIP RESOURCES
PO BOX 340003 • NASHVILLE, TN 37203-0003
www.discipleshipresources.org

Cover design by Anessa Magras.
Interior design by PerfecType, Nashville, TN.

ISBN 978-0-88177-533-4

Library of Congress Data-in-Publication on File

Table of Contents

Contributors

Editors

Valerie Bridgeman Davis, PhD, Biblical Studies (Hebrew Bible) teaches Old Testament, preaching and worship at Memphis Theological Seminary. She directs the Return Beat: Syncopating the Arts and Theology Institute at the MTS. Dr. Bridgeman Davis is the author of several books of poetry and her work appears frequently in womanist literature. She is in the process of completing several books on Old Testament hermeneutic. She and Dr. Ella Mitchell edited volume 5 of *Those Preaching Women* and Dr. Bridgeman Davis is the general editor of the 3-volume *Africana Worship Book* series.

Safiyah Fosua, DMin, is the Director of Invitational Preaching Ministries at GBOD in Nashville, Tennessee and a clergy member of the Greater New Jersey Annual Conference of the United Methodist Church. She is the author of several books and is associate editor of the 3-volume *Africana Worship Book* series. Dr. Fosua is a poet, a preacher and a devotional writer who writes weekly preaching and liturgical resources for the GBOD Worship Website (www.umcworship.org).

Contributors

Jeremiah A. Wright, Jr., DMin, is Senior Pastor of the 8000+-member Trinity United Church of Christ, the largest UCC congregation in the United States. Dr. Wright is in high demand as a visiting seminary professor is the author of several books and numerous articles including *What Makes You So Strong?* and *Good News! Sermons of Hope for Today's Families*. Dr. Wright is known on several continents as a world-class preacher and theologian with two earned master's degrees and seven honorary doctorates.

Pianapue Kept Early, DMin, the son of Methodist parents, is a Bassa United Methodist Christian from Liberia and a PhD Candidate at the University of Virginia. He currently serves as an adjunct Professor of Theology at Samuel DeWitt Proctor School of Theology, in Richmond, Virginia. Dr. Early is an elder in the Alabama West-Florida Conference.

Gennifer Benjamin Brooks, PhD, is Assistant Professor of Homiletics at Garrett-Evangelical Seminary and directs their Styberg Preaching Center. She has authored *Praise the Lord*, a book of liturgy, is completing a textbook on preaching and was a consultant for the *Zion Still Sings* songbook. Dr. Brooks is a native of Trinidad and an elder in the New York Annual Conference of the United Methodist Church.

William B. McClain, DMin, is the Mary Elizabeth McGehee Joyce Professor of Preaching at Wesley Theological Seminary in Washington, DC. In addition to his work in theology and homiletics, Dr. McClain has served as a consultant to both the *Songs of Zion* and the *Zion Still Sings* songbooks and is the author of *Come Sunday, the Liturgy of Zion* and *Black People in the Methodist Church: Whither Thou Goest?*

Cheryl Kirk-Duggan, PhD, is Assistant Professor of Theology and Women's Studies and Director of Women's Studies at Shaw University Divinity School in Raleigh, North Carolina. Dr. Kirk-Duggan is the author of numerous books in the areas of womanist biblical interpretation, gender studies, and worship with titles like *The Sky is Crying, Violence and Theology, Soul Pearls* and *African American Special Days*. Dr. Kirk-Duggan is an ordained elder in the Christian Methodist Episcopal Church.

Frank A. Thomas, DMin, is Senior Pastor of the 8,000-member Mississippi Blvd. Christian Church, in Memphis, Tennessee, and a PhD candidate at the University of Memphis. Dr. Thomas is the author several books including *They Like To Never Quit Praisin' God* and co-editor of *9.11.01 African American Leaders*

Respond to an American Tragedy. Dr. Thomas teaches in several MDiv, and DMin programs across the country and is known widely as CEO of *The African American Pulpit.*

Melinda Weekes, Esq., is a Gospel Music Theorist with Weekes in Advance Enterprises. Attorney Weekes is also a staff minister at the Bethel African Methodist Episcopal Church in Boston, Massachusetts.

Jessica Kendall Ingram, DMin, currently serves as the Supervisor for Women for the Tenth0 Episcopal District of the African Methodist Episcopal Church. Dr. Ingram, the author of a number of books on prayer and spiritual formation, was the first African American to be trained in Spiritual Direction at the Columbiere Center in Clarkston, Michigan.

Lisa Allen, PhD, is the Assistant Professor of Music and Worship at the Interdenominational Theological Seminary in Atlanta, Georgia. She chairs the Church Music and Worship department at the Interdenominational Theological Center in Atlanta and oversees their Master of Arts in Church Music degree program. Dr. Allen is completing two books on worship and is an elder in the North Georgia Conference of the United Methodist Church.

Otis Moss III, MDiv, serves as Pastor of Trinity UCC under Dr. Jeremiah A. Wright, Jr. He is a published author, and his essays, articles, and poetry appear in magazines across the country. Rev. Moss holds the distinction of being the youngest minister to speak at the Hampton University Minister's and Musicians Conference–on three occasions!

F. Douglas Powe, Jr., PhD, Assistant Professor of Evangelism at the St. Paul's School of Theology in Kansas City, Missouri, holds the E. Stanley Jones Chair in Evangelism. He is co-author of *Transforming Evangelism, the Methodist Way of Sharing Faith.* Dr. Powe, who serves on the National Advisory Committee for Spelman College, is an elder in the United Methodist Church.

Elonda Clay is a PhD student in Religion and Science at the Lutheran School of Theology at Chicago. Her research focus is in models of relationships for religion and technology. Elonda Clay is a Fund for Theological Education Doctoral Fellow and a United Methodist Church Woman of Color Scholar.

Henry H. Mitchell, D.D., is retired in Atlanta, Georgia after a long, distinguished career in the areas of history, homiletics, and Black Church Studies. Dr. Mitchell, often known as the godfather of black preaching, is author of several definitive works on black preaching, and black hermeneutics to include *Black Preaching, Preaching for Black Self-Esteem, and Soul Theology.*

Marilyn E. Thornton, MDiv, is the lead editor of African American resources at the United Methodist Publishing House and the Pastor of Spiritual Formation and Worship Arts at the South End United Methodist Church in Nashville, Tennessee. Rev. Thornton served as music editor for the recently release songbook, *Zion Still Sings.*

Wilma Taylor, MDiv, is working on a Master's of Public Health degree with an emphasis on psychosocial epidemiology at Walden University in Maryland. Rev. Taylor is an itinerant elder in the African Methodist Episcopal Church, currently serving as Associate Minister at the Grady-Madison AME Church in Madison, Alabama.

Linda H. Hollies, DMin, was known and loved as a prolific author, a profound speaker and a womanist scholar. She was, perhaps, best known for her *Trumpet in Zion* liturgy series and for numerous works addressing issues of domestic violence, incest and abuse, like *Inner Healing for Broken Vessels.* At the time of her death, Dr. Hollies was the Pastor of the Calvary United Methodist Church of Jackson, Michigan.

Acknowledgements

We gratefully acknowledge the generosity of the many scholars who wrote the articles contained in this book, of George Donigian and Doug Hagler of Discipleship Resources who recognized the value of this collection of writings, of Jean Musterman from the Center for Worship Resourcing who graciously handled the administrative details of our work together, of GBOD-UMC and Memphis Theological Seminary who blessed us and released us to collect and edit this volume, and of the Africana Cloud of Witnesses whose stories continue to unfold.

Introduction

VALERIE BRIDGEMAN DAVIS

We offer this volume of essays to help churches, professors, and students reflect more deeply on the work that we produced for Africana worship. These essays started out as small notes in the margins of the *Africana Worship Book, Year B.* We had the notion that we would interlace worship pieces with reflections from prominent leaders and thinkers in Africana life. We used North American leaders, not thinking much of the implication of that decision at the time. Even though we expected people to engage larger Africana realities, we believed our work would probably be used most on the North American continent. But what started out as a modest proposal turned out to be a larger enterprise.

We expected writers to create original articles. We discovered, however, there were articles already in print that suited our goals and have included them. Those reprinted pieces (at least one greatly revised for our purposes) include articles by William B. McClain, Cheryl Kirk-Duggan, Frank A. Thomas, Otis B. Moss III, Safiyah Fosua, and me. In addition, we accepted three sermons that we believe make clearly the connection between proclamation, worship, and living in Africana communities. The articles are arranged by what seems to be a natural flow, but they may in fact be treated independently of each other.

I revisit the **"21 Questions"** listed in the first *Africana Worship Book, Year A*[1]. Many people have said they were helpful tools. This article groups the concerns, not as the questions themselves, but as general issues each question tried to address.

The next article, **"Go Play with God: Reclaiming Liturgy for Spiritual Formation"** was included as the introduction to *Africana Worship Book, Year B*[2], and reflects my idea that whatever else we say about worship–specifically or broadly–I believe we have to learn to delight in God as One who wants to be connected with us; that we must return to the innocent play children brought to a playtime of worship–play that metamorphosed into a genuine encounter with divine presence.

This play is subversive in the gathered community, as co-editor Safiyah Fosua describes in her article **"Liturgy as Subversive Activity."** Using Africana worship pieces, she explains how the work we have produced has been deliberately "honest" and "real," meant to connect with people's lived realities. She used those pieces in workshop and connected liturgy, "words of defiance," to the prophetic work and words of Jesus. Our words, then, she insists, must propel us beyond the pews into a world where believers are willing to imagine the world that could be rather than the one that is. An adaptation of this article originally appeared in the accompaniment version of *The Upper Room Worship Book.*[3]

Jeremiah Wright's challenge for all Africana worship in **"To Serve This Present Age . . ."** is a reflection on a question of elders in the black church tradition: how are we connecting the dots between Africa and the Diaspora of Africa's children. He excoriates preaching that embraces a colonial, capitalistic imperialism (prosperity preaching) that forgets "the realities facing Africans on the Continent and Africans who languish under the heel of Free Market capitalism and First World greed." For Wright, preaching in the black church that is disconnected from our roots is antithetical to the gospel itself. If African American clergy, and I would add all Africana clergy throughout the world, are to serve "this present age," then it requires "reading those texts through the lenses of a people who understand what it means to be oppressed, a people for whom 'life ain't been no crystal stair' and it also means preaching faithfully to Africans living in Diaspora. It means preaching a word of hope and a word of heritage."

Fosua's article on **"Africana Theology for the Black Church"** expands Wright's concerns as she addresses the need to "san-ko-fa", "turn, go back, and pick it up," i.e., those parts of our African history that connect Diasporan Africans to the continent. She tells us that living as a missionary in Ghana helped her to fall in love twice over: with the Bible and with being black. The question is not what Christianity took away from Africans, but "What did they

(Africans) see in Christianity that had perhaps been overlooked by their captors?" Fosua argues that Africans recognize the worldview of the Bible because "we come from the world where the Bible was written." She persuasively argues that there is something "distinctly and identifiably African" about Blacks, no matter what denominational or religious affiliation. Africana theology then is an attempt to "wear our own eyeglasses."

Pianapue Kept Early's article, **"Worshipping Contextually: the Bassa People in the United Methodist Church in Liberia,"** offers an example of Wright's and Fosua's call to "connect the dots." He describes the way in which the choirs of the traditional Bassa church use the instruments of Africa–drums, tambourines, the harmonizing vocals–with sparse use of Western musical instruments. He says, "the role of the traditional choir is to provide a missing link: to give a cultural and spiritual flavor to the service, something that the hymns cannot invoke in the Bassa congregations." His article, **"Translatability as Belonging: Bassa United Methodist Christians in Liberia"** furthers the notion that for native Liberians, having songs like Amazing Grace, the creeds, and the Lord's Prayer translated into their language allowed them to embrace Christianity. Often at odds with the North American black transplants, these natives found in translation a connection with God and the church that continues to last.

Gennifer Brooks, in her essay **"The Creation of an Africana Worship Ritual: Baptism in the Shouters of Trinidad,"** discuss the ways in which Africana people in the Caribbean adapted Eurocentric worship symbols to create a uniquely Afrocentric celebration. Brooks lifts up the notion that these creations were essential to preserve the dignity of people "ripped from their religious and worship foundations. And these rituals that helped to preserve their identity served as a much-needed connection to their religious roots." Though we may have lost the historicity of some of the things Africana peoples do in worship throughout the world, Brooks aptly demonstrates that remnants remain for resource and remembrance.

Another "remnant" that melds black religious sensibilities with mainline protestant thinking is the word "circament," according to McClain. His article, **"The African American Church and Sacraments: But Can We Still Get Our 'Circament?'"** a reprint from Worship Arts, a publication of the Fellowship of United Methodists in Music and Worship Arts,[4] provides a historical look at a word unique to southern black worshipers, most notably Methodist Blacks. This word, "circament," probably is a cross between sacrament and circuit, to note that communion often was served only when a circuit rider elder came to town to administer the sacraments. In the article, McClain describes the importance of communion in black Wesleyan traditions.

Kirk-Duggan's article, **"Death as Worship: Celebrating Dying as Part of Life,"** is a reprint of a chapter from her book, *Refiner's Fire: A Religious Engagement with Violence.*[5] It provides an anchor for a discussion of the cycles of the liturgical year, and especially as the cycles relate to the death-dealing Africana people throughout the world must face–even as they continue to live. Using some of the most renowned Africana poets to reflect on death as worship, Kirk-Duggan skillfully leads us through the moments of ritual that matter for us. She says that the liturgical seasons provide us an opportunity to see the mystery and miracle of life and death. Using what she calls a "Womanist liturgics," Kirk-Duggan notes the power of language, suggesting our need to take care how we use words since life and death are in them. She says, "Womanist liturgics invite us to embrace and legitimize all hurting and pain, especially the grief process as ministry to the body of Christ. Womanist liturgics also celebrates and teaches us the values of balance. Thus as we cannot preach the entire Bible in one sermon, we cannot fully explore all the ramifications of life and death here."

It was fitting, then, that Frank A. Thomas sent us his article, **"The African American Funeral Sermon: Divine Re-Framing of Human Tragedy,"**[6] that first appeared in the *African American Pulpit* on funeral sermons. Since funerals are highly stylized rituals in most Africana settings, this essay demonstrated what Kirk-Duggan describes in her essay. Thomas begins with an episode about the death of a friend, and tells how the funeral ministered to him and his friends at the time. Though he could not say why, all these years later Thomas remembers that the funeral sermon "did something for us." Here he delineates the role of the preacher at a funeral as one that provides "a divine re-framing of human tragedy." In three moves, the preacher helps people face reality, see God's perspective, and then celebrate the good news of God's victory over death in general and over death in this particular situation. He says the preacher "celebrates the power of God to comfort, heal, and overcome death."

Thomas ends his essay recounting the celebratory moment of a funeral that included shouting and singing. Melinda Weeks writes about this singing that shapes the life and worship of Africans throughout the world in **"Music in Africana Worship."** She proclaims that "for Christian worshippers of the African Diaspora, music is the lifeblood of our communal experiences with God." She maintains that the centrality of music in Africana worship may be experienced no matter where Africans and their descendents are, whether Chicago or Carousal or Cape Town. She lifts up the diversity of this musical reality and speaks of the improvisation that mediates the "immediacy of God's presence in the midst of the assembly."

Jessica Kendall Ingram's sermon, **"Doxology in Darkness,"** helps address the constant question of theodicy that is not unique to Africana experience, but is persistent in it. Her sermon demonstrates what Thomas and Weekes describe as the enigmatic presence of God even in death and pain. Ingram lifts up the sense of absence believers, especially ministers, often feel as she connects her own struggle with the Psalmist's cry: *my God, my God, why have you forsaken me?* This sermon, preached during a women's conference, highlights choices people make to continue to worship while facing their "dark night." One of the things Thomas, Weekes, and Ingram lift up is the role music plays in any Africana theology.

In Lisa Allen's article, **"In the Spirit,"** she laments the loss of the use of hymnody and line singing in Africana congregation because "it's in the moaning, the groaning, the utterance too painful for words, that a hymn becomes the collective sigh and prayer of the people." She says there is a wealth of music being ignored and Allen rejects the notion that such songs are irrelevant, noting that worship is not intended to entertain, but rather bring the African American, the black church, to a God of justice and liberation. She does not reject, out of hand, new songs. Instead she hopes that "out of treasures old and new, we can build worship that acknowledge the changing culture, but does not lose the deep sigh of our ancestors."

By contrast, Otis Moss III proclaims in his hip-hop sermon, **"That Was Then, This Is NOW,"**[7] that Moses is dead. He wants the church to quit lamenting the "loss" of the old ways, and "remix" so that the elders are honored, but the methodologies of worship and prophetic preaching are attuned to a "postmodern, post-soul, post-civil rights, virtual-equipped generation." He calls on the congregation to understand that the church really is no longer the epicenter of the community. There are generations now who never knew Jim Crow in its late nineteenth, early twentieth-century forms. He notes that the problem with some churches is "we've got 8-track churches in a CD world," which is Moss' way of illustrating that we cannot use antiquated language or methods in the twenty-first century. This, he maintains, is the Joshua generation of laptops, dress-down, and Alicia Keys, not the Moses generation of Coltrane, Aretha, and handwritten letters. The sermon chides and confronts us, but also challenges and gives us courage that the church will make it in a hip-hop world that is more than gangsta rap; hip-hop is a mindset that must be understood and embraced.

Doug Powe puts Moss's sermon in a larger church context as he writes about the Emergent Church Movement. He notes in **"Emerging Possibilities for African American Worship"** that the movement is "an attempt to break modernity's hold on the church by moving away from rationalistic and individualistic ways of understanding Christianity." In other words, emerging worship embraces experience, relationships, and communities. It is more than "going to church" on Sundays. Emerging churches use art, dance, drama, small-group interaction and the like in order to address the cultural shift that undeniably happened in the late twentieth century to now. So, for Powe, the obvious connection with this larger church movement and the African/African American church is the hip-hop culture. Taking seriously Moss's sermon and critique from the Emerging Church Movement, Powe insists that African/African Americans already have the resources in the form of commitment from elders to produce "*griot-circles* where the past, present, and future learn from one another in the same room."

One of the places where "old school" and emerging churches meet is in the area of technology. Elonda Clay suggests, in **"Technologies for Worship,"** that churches think through the way they approach the ministry of technology and work to train or hire adequate support. She says that "before any equipment is purchased or a project using new technology is taken up, we might ask [this] question: Will this enhance the nurture, witness, and outreach of our congregation?"

None of these questions matter if in our worship we do not address the central question of the old spiritual and William McClain's article, **"Lord, How Come We Here?"** First printed as the foreword to the *Africana Worship Book, Year A*[8], his essay pushes us to this perennial question. The question, according to McClain, addresses the suffering and struggle of peoples who need a sense of worth and belonging. It leads to the affirmation in worship that "when the world beats us down, dismisses us as worthless, calls us everything else but a child of God, Africana spirituality reminds us that we are a chosen people." This spirituality and worship cannot be and must not be framed only in suffering, however; it includes "within its very fiber" justice and active grace, along with freedom and love.

The experience of this spirituality may be captured in "**Spiritual Focus and Africana Worship**." Preacher and Professor Henry Mitchell describes the sense of the ineffable role of the Spirit in ordering and directing worship. Mitchell calls this convergence "spiritual focus"–even if during times of planning people are unaware of just how much help God provides. He recalls an event in which he and his wife-preacher, Ella, preached together. The songs and prayers matched what they had prepared even though they had not conveyed their preaching texts or plans to the church. This conjoining of human hearts with heavenly fire can be missed, though. Mitchell says, "The greatest sins and shortcomings of the African American worship and preaching traditions occur at this point of spiritual focus." He laments our inability to wait on the Spirit to move, and the temptation to manufacture a response "by brute vocal simulation."

In her sermon, **"Worship: The Realm of the Spirit, the Realm of the**

Imagination, and Real Time," Marilyn Thornton maintains that we experience such lack of "spiritual focus" because we lack contemplative and retreat time. She captures the sense of the imaginative that is required to experience God, much as John did on the Isle of Patmos. A powerful example of the imaginative thinking and experience of God that Thornton argues for, the sermon stirs us to use our imagination. "It is through the imagination that creativity is stirred, producing real artistry, real solutions to problems, real new discoveries." She tells us the "imaginative" is the most real thing there is, since it is a gift of and from God and it should not be confused with imaginary, the un-real. She notes, "In imaginative, spiritual worship we take real time to bless God and give God the glory."

The way we use language is one place where the imaginative work that Thornton longs for may be addressed. In my article, **"Inclusive Language and Africana Worship,"** I argue that it is idolatrous to hold on to male-only language to describe humans and the Holy. The Bible has a number of metaphors by which we may speak of the Divine. I argue that "to box God into one metaphor (or one range of metaphors) and to insist that God cannot and ought not to be seen in any other way is to deny the radical freedom of God who may be whoever God wants to be and reveal Godself however God would." I recognize that God-language is hard for Africana communities to change because many Africana communities are functionally Unitarian, Jesus-only churches, while using Trinitarian formulas in liturgies. But I believe it is past time for us to move beyond limited and limiting language. We are called to struggle to freedom, even in our use of metaphors and imagination.

Few know the power of the imaginative spirituality better than Wilma Taylor, who in **"Testify!"** describes her battle with cancer and the role worship played and continues to play in her physical, emotional, and spiritual health. After the words from the doctor that brought her "heart pain and earache," Taylor embarked on a medical journey toward her health. Absence from a worshiping community during her treatment left her heartsick. The first time she was able to return to worship, a sermon on the raising of Lazarus sounded like a word straight to her own heart: "I felt that Jesus had called me from dark places of death to the light of life. It was Jesus who did the calling, and the community was the witness." As a health professional, Taylor is clear that the life-threatening cancer helped her experience worship differently. She says it caused her to "look to worship for wellness. It serves my wellness to be in the worship service. It serves my health to gather with others in the presence of God."

A number of writers have a "trinity" of what it means for black church to be black church Linda Hollies chose these three: women, music, and preaching in **"A Womanist Perspective on Spiritual Practices."** She starts with Eve and makes a case of how and where God has chosen and continues to choose women to ignite, lead, and inspire the church. Though women faced opposition, they still taught Bible in Sunday schools, vacation Bible schools, and mission departments. They raised money, sang and composed songs, and led choirs. She noted the advances women have made in the black church, citing the installation of Susan Johnson-Cook as the first woman to lead the 10,000-plus member Hampton Ministers' Conference. She was surrounded by women who conducted the installation without men leading, a signal for Hollies that "the women continue to lead the black church without apology." black women, she notes, have never failed to follow their call, even in the face of obstacles. Since Hollies died before this essay was published and her life was itself filled with many obstacles, her blessing at the end of the essay seems appropriate and prescient:

> Focus on God. Give service in the name of Jesus Christ. Allow your gifts to be used by the power of the Holy Spirit and make a permanent, positive impact where you are located today! May it be so now and forever, for it is the divine will of The Ancient of Days!

Notes

[1] Valerie Bridgeman Davis and Safiyah Fosua (eds.), *The Africana Worship Book, Year A* (Nashville, TN: Discipleship Resources, 2006).
[2] Valerie Bridgeman Davis and Safiyah Fosua (eds.), *The Africana Worship Book, Year B* (Nashville, TN: Discipleship Resources, 2007).
[3]Elise Eslinger, *The Upper Room Worship Book, Accompanist and Worship Leader Edition* (Nashville, TN: Upper Room Books, 2007).
[4] William B. McClain, The Importance of Holy Communion: The African American Church and the 'Circament'" in *Worship Arts*, March-April 1997, pages 8-11.
[5] Cheryl Kirk-Duggan, *Refiner's Fire: A Religious Engagement with Violence* (Minneapolis, MN: Augsburg Fortress, 2000).
[6] Frank A. Thomas, "The African American Funeral Sermon: Divine Re-Framing of Human Tragedy," *The African American Pulpit,* Volume 4, Number 1, Winter, 2000-2001.
[7] Otis M. Moss, III "That Was Then, This is NOW" in *The African American Pulpit,* Volume 10, Number 1, Winter 2006-2007.
[8] Valerie Bridgeman Davis and Safiyah Fosua (eds.), *The Africana Worship Book, Year A* (Nashville, TN: Discipleship Resources, 2006).

21 Questions Revisited

VALERIE BRIDGEMAN DAVIS

In the first *Africana Worship* volume, I listed twenty-one questions I believe worship leaders and planners might consider when preparing liturgy. Since the volume appeared, we have received feedback that the questions were helpful and used over and over by groups discussing and planning worship. I first drafted the list during a writing consultation as we tried to figure out what we meant by *Africana worship*. It seemed to me that there were compelling concerns that needed to be addressed, regardless of the worship setting.

1. Is the worship biblically resonated?
2. Is the worship theologically sound?
3. Is it ritually profound?
4. Is worship invitational?
5. Is this worship contextually relevant? Does worship reflect the culture(s), lands, and peoples gathered for worship?
6. Does the worship open an aperture to the presence of God? Have we created space for God to work and speak and encounter us, and us God?

7. Is the worship participatory? Or, are there simply "talking heads" upfront that we may "tune out"?
8. Does worship pull people from the outer edges into the center?
9. Does worship incorporate gifts from the larger church (worldwide) into our local context?
10. Does this worship challenge our local context to be a witness of God through the holy, catholic (universal) church? Does the worship " prophesy" a more inclusive reality than the one the congregation currently knows?
11. Did we leave appropriate space for stillness and silence?
12. Does worship incarnate God in Christ, begging participants to be reconciled to God?
13. Do the words of the liturgy bog down and drown out rhythm and mystery of the liturgy? Or, are litanies and prayers easy to enter, with refrains and rhythms that hold the central message in place? Is there a "heartbeat" (rhythm) worshippers can carry beyond this "thin line" moment?
14. Is worship hermetically sealed? Does it have one way in and one way out, and is it over when it's over, not carrying worshipers into the world to continue to praise, worship, repent, grow, and work?
15. Is worship permeable? Are there several entry points into Divine mystery and is it portable into the rest of the worshiper's life?
16. Is worship democratic? Does it allow voices from the center and the margin to commingle in such a way that there is no clear dominant voice? Have we invited the communion of saints from the beginning of the church's existence to the present day to speak? Do we have a word from the Old Testament, the New Testament, and the Now Testament? Do we believe God continues to speak?
17. Does the music we sing, pray, and dance reflect the reality of more than a "village" God? Are we creating theology by our worship that says God is truly the God of all universes, places, and times?
18. Did we use technology wisely and economically? Did we allow the "bells and whistles" to get in the way of the simplicity of grace?

19. Is worship visionary and prophetic? Does this worship service point us to God of the whole creation, God who loves diversity in color and sunsets, in temperature and foliage? In mountains and valleys, in rushing waterfall and gentle-flowing brooks?
20. Is worship sensory-rich? Does worship use art in ways that God is danced back into the consciousness of people? Do we sing God into the room? Do we vision God into the room with banners and clips? Do we act God into the room?
21. Does this worship return us to the miracle of hearing on the day of Pentecost, and to the great celebration around the throne of God when the reign of God is fully and completely realized and we out of every tongue, language, tribe, nation, gender, and age, lift our voices in awesome wonder of God who is majestic, powerful, holy, generous, friend, glorious, wonderful, and worthy of all this worship?

Revisiting those questions, I now see that they can be grouped into some general categories. Looking back, I see these questions might be reduced to five or expanded to fifty, depending on how in-depth one wants to be. The goal, of course, is to get congregations and worship planners to think deeply, to consider seriously, and to pray about the pause that gathered worship represents.

In this essay, I do not list the questions one by one, but rather reconsider the concerns I intended to address in them. Those concerns, as I see them now, include biblical content in worship, theological integrity, pastoral concerns, prophetic energy, authenticity, ecumenism, intercessory passion, spiritual openness, and ritual richness.

The first question, "is the worship biblically resonated," did not mean and still does not mean whether or not the litany or call uses actual scripture. Instead, I tried to impress upon writers (and by extension planners) that the biblical story and words are located in the bones of Bible-believing people. As such, phrases like "God of widows and orphans" or "Seeking God" sound like the Bible to people. That is, people recognize the God these words reflect, and remember they have heard them somewhere. Having "biblically resonating" words allows the writer or planner to also use words native to the context in which they live–so people will recognize the extra-canonical words of popular culture married to biblical phrases. The dialogue between the biblical world and the worshipers' world provides the space for theological inquiry.

Theological integrity means worship pushes worshipers to go beyond merely mouthing liturgical words; the worship design drives people to consider issues of justice (are we creating theology that says God is truly God of all universes, places, and times, #17; also 2, 5). Does worship reflect the God of Pentecost, and a vision of a world reconciled to God? This concern, in fact, permeated all the questions in my mind.

When people gather, they come weary, battered, hopeful, needy, and in so many other human states of being. Worship must discern, in its shape, how to meet the pastoral needs of those gathered, while provoking worshipers beyond themselves. Meditations, prayers, and litanies, for example, express very real human conditions, authentically and unapologetically describing pain, hopelessness, anger, and sadness while declaring God's good news. Pastoral concerns acknowledge that worshipers gather to be "leaning posts" for one another, in black church vernacular. When people receive a benediction and leave the confines of the worship space, they should believe that those who led them cared deeply about their lives and that they wanted for them what God wants.

Whatever pastoral means, it does not mean that people are not challenged to "heal the world." Worship may be shaped to reflect concerns for all creation, for people in other lands, and for the whole church. These concerns are prophetic. Worship should call people with power to accountability; comfort those who are oppressed, and empower oppressed people to revolutionize their own lives, with the help of God. In order to get everyone present to participate in the prophetic ministry of the church, worship, of necessity, must be participatory. Participation in worship allows people to practice in the gathered community that which is the people's worship in the world. So, I asked whether worship was hermetically sealed, over when it's over, "not carrying worshipers into the world to continue to praise, worship, repent, grow, and work" (#14).

For me, ecumenism is one dimension of prophetic energy. Jesus prayed that his disciples would live in unity. A glance around the globe shows us a fractured church. One way that worship can help reflect our prayer for unity as we work for it is that we sing and pray as we "incorporate gifts from the larger church (worldwide) into our local context" (#9) and "challenge our local context to be a witness of God through the holy, catholic (universal) church . . . [and] 'prophesy' a more inclusive reality than the one the congregation currently knows" (#10). Churches still may be mono-cultural, but our singing, our litanies, etc., may borrow from the larger church as testimony to our relationship and our commitment to unity and solidarity. Ecumenism and prophetic witness go hand in hand.

Intercessory passion is another dimension of ecumenism and prophetic witness. We pray with deep concern and fervor for the church, the world, and all creation when we believe God is at work. Prayer is the church's primary work, even when those prayers are with our feet and hands. The church is Christ's intercessory presence in the world. On some level, each question begs worshipers to pray.

The bulk of the questions reflect my concern for the twins, "spiritual openness" and "ritual richness," because I believe all the aforementioned issues can find their voice when these two ideas are addressed. These concerns demand that simplicity not get drowned in bells and whistles; that worship is sensory-rich; that worship is profound, rather than mundane or profane; that worship "open an aperture to the presence of God" where we "create space for God to work and speak and encounter us, and us God" (#6).

When we consider these categories, worship then becomes authentic and fully embodied by a local congregation. As such, local congregations will find their prophetic voice, own their theology contextualized by the realities of the lives they lead and the lives they touch, and be aware of their relationship with the global church. Whether the questions contract or expand for planners, when taken seriously, they lead us into an abiding relationship with God who so loves the world. Liturgies that prayerfully lead us to the world-loving God are sound, biblically, theologically, pastorally, and prophetically.

Go Play with God: Reclaiming Liturgy for Spiritual Formation[1]

VALERIE BRIDGEMAN DAVIS

I grew up in the 1960s and '70s in the country–really. I grew up in Alabama, forty miles southeast of Birmingham between Childersburg and Sylacauga. We lived on land that was on my grandfather's farm. Many of my cousins lived in the area. We were each other's playmates. My mom and grandparents would put us out of the house after the chores were done, the eggs were gathered, any cotton picked or chopped that we were required to do, any peas shelled. We were dismissed with the command, "GO PLAY."

"GO PLAY" took on the form of many activities, but the one that I want to tell you about is when we "played church." My grandfather was a deacon in a Baptist Church and, until we were teenagers, we grew up in Pine Grove Baptist church in Odena. So "play church" for us took on a Baptist flavor. We would draw straws to see who was going to be the preacher, who would be the soloist, who would be the old lady that was going to faint after she shouted. As children, we always included Communion when we played church. We would get a slice of Wonder Bread and cups of strawberry Kool-Aid for the elements.

The preacher would get to a fever pitch; we would all pretend to be "happy;" the preacher would do the call to repentance; one of us would "give our heart to God and our hand to the preacher." Then give an invitation to the table.

The best I can remember, we always did: "Come everyone who is thirsty; come to the water and you who have no money, come buy and eat". It's a passage from Isaiah 55 and I honestly don't know why we knew it because the preacher in our local congregation always did "on the night in which Jesus was betrayed" from 1 Corinthians 11. We would, as children, wax eloquent about how God could quench your thirst AT THE TABLE; how God could feed your soul AT THE TABLE. We'd get happy all over again and then receive the elements.

Sometimes our Gran-Gran would catch us "playing church," and with much consternation she would say to us: "Ya'll better quit playing with God." QUIT PLAYING WITH GOD. Ya'll quit playing with God. Sheepishly, we would pack up our makeshift worship space, gulp down our "red" Kool-Aid, eat whatever bread was left, and go off to "hide-and-seek" or some other game that was acceptable to our grandmother.

I've thought about the admonition over the years: "Ya'll quit playing with God," and now that I'm older and teaching seminarians worship and preaching, I respectfully disobey. If anything, I am ready to tell the church, "Ya'll, come play with God."

Liturgy, "the work of the people," is playing with God. For me, liturgy is where our playful hearts meet the creative imagination of God and God experiences worship while we experience grace, redemption, re-formation, salvation, and wholeness. Worship belongs to God. It is in our play: our proclamation, our affirmations, and our repetitive recitation of the truths of our faith that we meet the God of all creation, God who spoke and still speaks. We play on the edges of eternity, seeking to know the incomprehensible, unknowable One.

Worship, then, is an encounter with a playful God in a playing creation. The gathering of the people of God for this worship is an aperture, an opening in the midst of ordinary life, in which we slip the sacred completely on (please note that I said "completely on" as I believe all life and living is sacred, every event is an opportunity of worship, from washing dishes to studying to making love with your beloved).

We gather to continue what we've already been doing; only in our gathering we make a larger space for God than is normally in our day-to-day grind. We pull back the curtain, the thin veil between heaven and earth and confess our own neediness to stop and to be more fully aware of God, who is always and everywhere present with us. The gathering of the people of God is not a "start-and-stop" event; that is, we do not "start" worship and then "end" worship, rather we more intentionally worship in a broader space with God and we send each other back into our lives worshipping. This pausing in the midst of worship, this standing still just to acknowledge our neediness, our desperation for another drink of water from the fountain of life, from the well of salvation, this moment is, and always is, a God-moment. In these moments we are reshaped, remolded into the form that our potter first formed us: we experience spiritual reformation in the liturgical moment.

Marva Dawn[2] speaks of a liturgical hermeneutic, that is, a way of interpreting all of our lives, all of the scripture (word of God) in just such a way that it leads us to worship and to reformation. Liturgy is as much proclamation as is preaching and sacraments. Liturgy has an inherent power to spiritually form us. I want to think further about this spiritual reformation.

I contend that much of the malaise and the morass in our congregations, whether they are United Methodists, Church of God, Baptists, or otherwise, may be traced to our inattention to this liturgical work. We are too careless in our pause, in our gathering. We treat these moments as intrusions rather than necessary interruptions. We gather from habit and occupy our minds with what's for dinner or what game is on (even those of us charged with leading people into the palpable presence of God); we are often out of the room when we worship and the gathering is rote and resisted because we do not understand.

What is it we don't understand? We neither understand the depth of our own neediness nor God's desire to fill us with God's own self. That first recognition of neediness has to begin with those tasked with planning for this interruption, the holy "hold-up." If the worship team and the pastor do not understand themselves to be "the neediest people in the room," then they will grab a hymnal or the latest CD by the most popular gospel singer and the lectionary texts and throw something together, presuming that the shape of the worship is incidental to the "real thing," i.e., the preaching. Or they will simply presume people don't care about the liturgy. We project onto the awaiting congregation our own disregard for structure and communal words and movements. This hodgepodge way of pulling together the worship event–even when it appears to be deliberate and thoughtful–is a result of not understanding that the liturgy forms us whether we plan for it to do so or not. If we understood the depth of our own neediness, we would turn this task over a thousand ways, asking "what do we need to be truly God's offering to the world?" "What do we need to be prophetic and proactive in this world?" "What do we need to be whole and redemptive?" "What do we need, really, to please God and to be coworkers and co-creators with God in Christ Jesus in this world?" These questions would push us to the limits. We would not choose songs for their titles, but rather to answer the question: "What does God want to form in us today?" We would not choose the Nicene Creed "just because;" but rather we would consider which creedal statement of the church, or whether a new creedal statement of the church, is necessary for today's formation. The liturgy with its fourfold design: gathering, word, intercessions, sending–would always be formed around these kinds of questions. We would ponder how these people gathered here and now, must be formed for their particular vocation. We would seek a word for this group, right here. (The planners would say by their planning, "We thought about you: who you would be, from where you would come, what you would have left behind to be here, to what you will return, why you came. We thought about how we struggle to make relevant the mysteries of our faith or at least to make this present in a real way.")

In addition we would have to ask, not only "what do we need," but also with what does God desire to fill us. What is God's desire? When is the last time we really asked that question? What does God desire, not "require" as in Micah 6:8, which we are quick to quote and less quick to live, but what does God *desire*? Have you ever thought about the passionate God we serve? Have you ever reflected on just how much God loves us, and how intensely? Have you ever wondered what we would be if we ever got the revelation that God is SO in LOVE with US creatures, great and small? That God really meant, "That's good" and "that's very good."

It took me awhile to be delivered from "worm" theology. Yes, I know we are corrupted by sin and broken under its weight; yes, I know all creation is groaning for redemption–I groan internally myself. Yes, I know that we are prone to wander (LORD, I *feel* it), prone to leave the God we love. But I also am persuaded that nothing can or will separate us from the love of God. *Persuaded.* "Persuasion" is a word we don't use often.

I had a friend ask me as he was preparing to go to the battlefield in Iraq in 2003: "What would you do if you weren't afraid of God." I quickly answered (and meant it): I am not afraid of God. I believe that I can do anything and I mean ANYTHING I want to do and it would not for *one minute* have an impact on God's love for me. It is knowing this radical, extravagant, prodigal (as in wasteful) love that compels me and constrains me to a loving relationship that is grounded less in obedience and grounded more in a mad, crazy love relationship. This kind of relationship, I think, is what God desires. If God desires this kind of relationship with us, then when we pause for a more intentional encounter, how is our worship shaping this love relationship? How does our worship frame God's love for those who are accustomed to thinking of God as an angry, easily provoked, wrathful God and not as a lover who longs for relationship, a lover whose heart can be broken when the beloved refuses to return this love–or when the beloved siphons off his or her love so that there is little or none left for God, so that God gets leftovers. So, when we gather, I believe the liturgy should reshape us with these two things in mind: our neediness and God's desire.

How does that liturgical shaping look? Let me go back to my story about us playing as children. I told you how we would draw straws to see who would preach and do Communion. Unbeknown to us we were creating a hunger for the Word spoken and the Word consumed, and ultimately for the Word lived. Divine intervention in our playfulness taught us instinctively that Word spoken and Word consumed were integral to encountering God. Many times as children we would cross over into *we're not playing anymore* and experience God's presence. Sometimes we had words for that encounter; more often we would just look at each other and stare, unable to articulate this inbreaking of Spirit on little children. Our freedom to explore and to believe, really, that there is God, I believe made us easy spiritual targets. God moved on and in us.

We, to be sure, probably weren't very doctrinally savvy. We probably just parroted much of what we had heard from our pastors. But often we would become our own theological selves and imagine what a scripture meant, pray that scripture over one another then use it at the Table of the Lord. Remember, we were playing. But now, I would say: we were playing, but God wasn't. I was, and my cousins and siblings were, formed in those moments as much as we were in Sunday school and in Sunday morning worship. We were learning without knowing that we were learning. We were being shaped by the unseen hand of a Potter, our clay not yet hardened by boredom or tradition or checking out, presuming that worship wasn't necessary. I know we were being shaped primarily because I think about how often we returned to "playing church." It was as much a favorite pastime as playing cops-and-robbers, cowboys-and-Indians, and aliens from another planet. This "playing church" and "playing with God" helped make us into the people we were becoming.

I wonder what would happen if we leaders–the neediest people in the room–recognized that we are being formed in the liturgical moment. I wonder what would happen if we took seriously our call to think and plan theologically for the gathering, and think about what we are saying in our words and actions, at the table and at the door? What would happen if we knew, really knew, that the desperation people feel is a desperate need for God in Christ Jesus? What would happen if we reclaimed the liturgy as a place in which God shapes us into a vessel God can use?

At Memphis Theological Seminary, I teach students representing more than thirty Christian denominations, but a great majority of my students are in process as Methodist ministers. Many of them already are serving small congregations, sometimes two and three or more churches at one time. These students often tell me that in their contexts, mostly rural and small, the people are resistant to liturgy. They want to do what they've already been doing. They find the resources of the church not very helpful, and on it goes. These students complain that in their Methodist congregations the local Baptist flavor rules the day and that except for the name on the door, you can't even tell they are of the Wesleyan tradition. They tell me that the liturgy shapes them differently from the confessions to which they claim allegiance.

I am always curious about these conversations. When I begin to ask students what they are doing to reshape the liturgy to be consistent with the confessions of the United Methodist Church, they quickly tell me that people don't want to change. When I press them into the notion that the Methodist church is a connectional communion and presumes that they will together keep a discipline and be guided by a book of order, many of these student-pastors tell me people don't care about the book of order, except when they want to get rid of a pastor. And, that people most want to get rid of a pastor when that pastor messes with the way things always have been. Pressed even further, I finally arrive at what I've already suspected: these pastors themselves don't want to think too much about liturgy, don't care to use "written" and "boring" forms from the United Methodist hymnal; or they are battle weary and don't want to fight. Or–gasp–these student-pastors don't care about form as a functional part of how God changes us.

So I find the first resistance, the first barriers through which we must break are in leaders themselves. What if we could convince leaders there is life in "them there forms?" What if we could convince leaders that this order has a way of giving people a container by which to contemplate the mysteries of God, that the intercessions and the calls to the table, that the confessions and the professions of faith, that the preaching and the singing, all lead us more fully into the presence of almighty God. What if we could convince leaders that this "work of the people" leads to spiritual transformation?

I must confess that sometimes I leave the semester worn out from trying to convince people they should either be who they claim to be or go to another spiritual expression. It matters, though, to me. While denominations may not be God's best, denominations give us containers by which we can articulate the things we most surely believe. And though any particular communion may be a wide tent, it still has a canopy that defines it. This truth is what I struggle to impress upon my students.

The litanies, calls to worship, petitions, and the like of the Africana Worship Book series are designed to help leaders move congregations from resistance to renewal in liturgical forms. They are of a particularly Africana flavor. The best we really are able to do is "salt" our hearts to raise a thirst level for forms and functional words that will lead the people of God into an encounter that will not end with amen, but one that will lead them on until they pause again for the call to *come.* The best we may do is examine what words, what movements, what texts and prayers will form us into the image of Christ, how we may be to the world the body of Christ, broken and poured out on its behalf. The best we may do is make an offering that brings us closer to the Mystery, in the word sung, in the word prayed, in the word proclaimed, in the word at the table, and in the word sending us out into God's future.

The Africana Worship Book series continues our commitment to find the heartbeat of people on the African continent and those scattered from it. It represents our hope to find the words that follow the liturgy in a lively and Spirit-filled way. It also is our offering for sustenance on the road to God. Welcome to the journey. Peace.

Valerie

Notes

[1] A first version of this essay was presented at the "This Holy Mystery: Teaching the Sacrament/Improving our Practice," opening plenary, April 26–28, 2005. The article later served as the Introduction to *The Africana Worship Book, Year A.*

[2] Marva Dawn, *Reaching Out Without Dumbing Down: A Theology of Worship for this Urgent Time* (Grand Rapids, MI: Wm. B. Eerdmans Publishing Company, 1995).

Liturgy as Subversive Activity[1]

SAFIYAH FOSUA

Once, for a brief worship time that preceded a workshop on contextual preaching, I used several liturgies that had been written by participants in the 2004 Africana liturgy consultation. A call to worship reflected candidly on the needs and shortcomings of any group of people who gather. A litany reminded us that those who were living on the streets were also on God's mind. A benediction challenged workshop participants to take a loving look at the people of their community. At the end, I asked participants to share their honest opinions of the contextual liturgies that they had just spoken. One woman smiled and said: these words were *honest.* Another observed that she felt appropriately challenged to pay more attention to people in her neighborhood and their needs. Still another felt the connection between worship and daily living.

The liturgies used for that short opening worship accomplished their purpose. We drew near to God. We voiced our collective prayers and concerns about troubling situations. We affirmed our commitment to participate in the work of God. And, more specifically, we made the connection between our "time with God" and daily life. In less than thirty minutes, we made the existential leap from complacency about the poor and disenfranchised among us to a commitment to do *something* on their behalf. We went from accepting this world's standards to yearning for the inbreaking of the world to come. You might say what happened in that room was subversive.

Nearly ninety years ago, James Weldon Johnson stood the literary world on its ear by publishing *The Creation* in 1918. Now it is a sacred literature masterpiece narrated by great orators like James Earl Jones. But ninety years ago, things were quite different. James Weldon Johnson envisioned his task this way: "to find a form that will express the racial spirit by symbols from within rather than by symbols from without . . . A form that is freer and larger than dialect . . . ."[2] What was so shocking? Was it the shock of imagining God through the eyes of black peoples or was it that Johnson, representing a whole ethnic group, dared to see himself created in the image of God? Either way, this piece of sacred liturgy, canonized by the black community, is an example of liturgy as communal (subversive) witness.

No Ease in Zion

History teaches us that the people of God are rarely comfortable with the way things are. Shortly after Jesus began his public ministry, he informed us of several of his goals for ministry in the well-known declarations of Luke 4.

> "The Spirit of the Lord is upon me, because he has anointed me to bring good news to the poor. He has sent me to proclaim release to the captives and recovery of sight to the blind, to let the oppressed go free, to proclaim the year of the Lord's favor" (Luke 4:18–19 NRSV).

While appearing to be an innocent recap of Isaiah 61, Jesus' words were subversive. His words hinted that poverty and oppression were not acceptable to God. Jesus' words hinted at the principles of Jubilee that the people had repeatedly failed to observe. Jubilee was intended, once every fifty years, to level the economic playing field–a time when property reverted to the original owners and debts were forgiven. By proclaiming the year of the Lord's favor Jesus was certain to get into trouble with the rich, the powerful, and anyone with a vested interest in the established order–especially after it became evident that he was willing to risk death in order to turn the world right side up!

The good news of the gospel has a decided air of subversion embedded in its language and liturgies. Gabriel's Annunciation to Mary and the subsequent Magnificat have subversive elements: *Greetings favored one, the Lord is with you!*

These words were spoken to a person who, before that moment, may not have felt particularly favored. Mary was a young girl from a poor family, living in an occupied country, learning how to take her place among the disenfranchised. It would have been just as easy for Mary to rear back on her heels, look the angel squarely in the face, and say: *"You ain't from around here are you?"* But that's not the way the story goes. God broke the rules of power etiquette and sent an angel to a peasant. Then, Mary refused to stay in her place; she accepted the challenge. There, in the presence of God, Mary and the angel spoke words back and forth to one another about things yet to come in the Reign of God–the angel, insisting the subversive: you *are* blessed and favored by God and, later, Mary saying subversive things about a God who scatters the proud and brings down oppressive rulers. Ironically, we often miss the scandal of the encounter when we repeat the words of the "Hail Mary" or the "Magnificat."

The early church's liturgy is filled with defiant words. Remember, *Thy kingdom come, thy will be done on earth as it is in heaven* was a prayer taught to people who endured Roman occupation and oppression under the hands of their own religious leaders. Similarly, the creedal declaration that Jesus overcame death, stormed the region of the dead, and rose again as proof of God's power and authority is subversive language!

Liturgy is more than rehearsed revelations about God from people who belong to the cloud of witnesses. Sometimes, liturgy is the subversive declaration of the coming Reign of God. The words of liturgy speak of both the Reign of God within the human soul and the coming Reign of God across the land. We are created in the image of the God who dares to speak of things that do not exist as though they already did (Romans 4:17). What might happen if *we* spoke more frequently of God's hopeful future in times of public and private worship?

Notes

[1] This article initially appeared in *The Upper Room Worship Book, Accompanist and Worship Leader Edition*, edited by Elise Eslinger and published by Upper Room Books in 2007 and is reprinted by permission.

[2] James Weldon Johnson, *God's Trombones, Seven Negro Sermons in Verse* (Toronto: Penguin Books, 1990), 8.

To Serve This Present Age . . .

Jeremiah A. Wright, Jr.

In Charles Wesley's hymn, "A Charge to Keep I Have," Wesley issues the following challenge to those of us who would dare say "Yes" to the awesome call to ministry that God places upon our lives:

> To serve this present age
> My calling to fulfill,
> Oh, may it all my powers engage
> To do my Master's Will[1].

African American clergy have been called to *serve the present age* in which they were called to do ministry ever since the seventeenth century in this country. African American clergy served their *present age* in the seventeenth century in North America as Africans in bondage.

They served as *griots* and as holders and keepers of the "sacred mystery" God had entrusted into their care. Many of their spiritual powers, their stories and their positions are captured in the African folklore that is the repository of our saga and sojourn in this country. The story of "Kuli ba!" from the Georgia seacoast Island of St. John's is one such story that talks about the African American clergy and the importance of their role (in their *present age*) prior to the war between the states that ended Chattel Slavery in the United States.

In the eighteenth century, the African American clergy who were called to serve the age in which they lived have names that are *legion*. From the African clergy in the Americas who led revolts in Haiti, in Surinam, in the Maroon communities in the Caribbean, and in the Deep South here in the United States, there is one long list of men and women who served the age in which God called them. Our record-keeping limits the luminaries' names to an isolated view in the eighteenth century, but we do have a record of black clergy like Richard Allen, Jarena Lee, Absalom Jones, George Liele, and Peter Varrick. There are countless others, however, who served beside them and whose names have been lost to antiquity, because we did not *tell our own story* in writing.

In the nineteenth century, the list of African American clergy who served the age in which they lived increases by quantum leaps. From Gabriel Prosser, Denmark Vesey, Nat Turner, and David Walker in the early 1800s up through Harriet Tubman (an African American Methodist Episcopal Zion minister) and Gordon Blaine Hancock, William Seymour and Charles Albert Tindley, the African American clergy who heard the voice of God and who served those who lived in their time there is an awesome list of heroes and sheroes, and every African American child needs to learn, memorize, internalize and pass on that list of names to unborn generations.

The twentieth-century list of black clergymen and black clergywomen is a list so long that just to spend one or two pages on each one of them would produce a book (a tome!) of over 1000 pages.

From Bishop Charles Harrison Mason and the Azusa Street Revival in the early 1900s through Adam Clayton Powell, Sr., Adam Clayton Powell, Jr., Samuel DeWitt Proctor, Gardner Taylor, Bishop Barbara Harris, Dr. Martin Luther King, Jr., Sandy Ray, Frederick G. Sampson, Prathia Hall-Wynn, Jacqueline Grant, Vashti McKenzie, Ann Lightener, Cynthia Hale, Johnnie Coleman, Barbara King, Carolyn Knight, Cheryl Sanders, Kelly Brown-Douglas, Safiyah Fosua, Gina Stewart and Reverend Susan Smith, the names and ministries of those African American clergy who have preached the gospel to God's people in their age in an uncompromising manner is absolutely incredible.

Otis Moss, Jr., Otis Moss, III, Fred Shuttlesworth, Ralph Abernathy, Walter Fauntroy, Jeremiah A. Wright, Sr., John Bennett Henderson, Charles Copher, Randy Bailey, Jerome Ross, John Kinney, Henry Mitchell, Ella Mitchell, J. Alfred Smith, Mack King Carter, Wyatt Tee Walker, James Forbes and James Cone–those names hardly put a dent in the "great cloud of witnesses" who stand tall and loom large as persons who lived faithfully and with integrity as they answered the call of God to serve the *present age* in which God blessed them to be born.

This one article and this one essay do not allow me the time and space to capture the importance of the African American preacher in this *Companion to the Africana Worship Book.* I would like to offer my observations, therefore, as an introduction to this important segment of what black preaching and what black worship have meant (and continue to mean) in the story of the African church in the United States of America.

W.E.B. DuBois said, in 1903, that there are three key ingredients to the black church. They are preaching, music, and the Holy Spirit. If you were to take any one of those three elements away you would no longer have the African American church. What you would have is a social club or a civic club.

Preaching is key to black worship! To shape my reflection around the importance of preaching for this essay, however, I will move away from DuBois' observation and use the combined (and distilled) wisdom of Dr. Gardner C. Taylor, Dr. Samuel DeWitt Proctor, Dr. James Forbes, and Dr. Otis Moss, Jr. Dr. Taylor offered us a word of caution in terms of our "preachments" in the twenty-first century in a presentation that he made at the Morehouse School of Religion and the Interdenominational Theological Center's Conference on African American clergy persons, confronting the various issues in ministry in *this present age.*

In the segment of the three-day seminar that dealt with the African American preacher as public theologian, Dr. Gardner C. Taylor threw down the gauntlet for those of us who dare try to serve *this present age.* He wondered out loud whether or not the African American clergy and African American churches would turn their backs on Africa in the twenty-first century in the same way that the African American clergy and church had turned their backs on Africa going into the twentieth century!

The question he raised with the clergypersons, theologians, seminarians, and attendees of the Conference was this: Will the gospel of Jesus Christ that we preach speak to the reality of Africans on the Continent and Africans who live in Diaspora as sons and daughters of an African heritage? Or will we buy into a prosperity gospel that has nothing to do with the realities facing Africans on the Continent and Africans who languish under the heel of Free Market capitalism and First World greed?

Because of the weight of white supremacy in the nineteenth century and the constant bombardment of negative images of Africa dumped on people of African descent in the United States of America, as Africans living in the late 1800s and early 1900s so painfully demonstrated, the average black Christian wanted nothing to do with Africa. We turned our back on our homeland!

Many African Americans in the early days of the twentieth century went so far as to remove the word "African" from the name of their churches and the thrust of their ministries!

Churches that had once been called (from their inception) First *African* Baptist Church, Second *African* Baptist Church and St. Thomas *African* Episcopal Church had their names changed in the twentieth century because the word "African" got to be "problematic" for Blacks who wanted nothing to do with Africa!

We changed the name of our churches to reflect the street on which we sat (12th Street Baptist Church, etc.), or we changed the name of our churches to make them sound "more biblical" as in "Mt. Zion Baptist Church." Halfway through the twentieth century, the Africans who worshipped in the historic St. Thomas African Episcopal Church in Philadelphia took the word "African" out of their official name. They went and had the charter changed so they would not be identified as Africans! (Fortunately, a younger group of conscious African Anglicans decided that the power and the importance of that crucial piece of history could not be done away with because of middle-class Negro fantasies about "integration" and the African community of St. Thomas once again embraces its African heritage.)

As Dr. Taylor raised that crucial issue I began to reflect on how many references to Africa I had heard and was hearing in the sermons of those who preached to African American congregations. Almost none of our mega-preachers touch Africa. Just as the ABC-TV special pointed out that our mega-preachers who address the largest number of African Americans in Diaspora do not touch the subject of HIV/AIDS among African Americans in their sermons, a parallel reality is that their sermons also do not "connect the dots" for Africans who live in Diaspora between the realities of living in Africa and the realities of living in a system of white supremacy in the United States of America. *We have turned out backs on our mother!*

Dr. Taylor also lifted up the fact that was further developed by Otis Moss, Jr., (and Dr. Samuel DeWitt Proctor and Dr. Miles Jerome Jones) in terms of the social content of the messages heard from the black pulpit. The social content, which cannot neglect the African hermeneutic and the reality of race in the twenty-first century, is painfully missing from all of the "name it and claim it, grab and nab it, tag it and bag it" pap preachments that we hear from the pulpits of those who are robbing Peter to pay the preacher!

Otis Moss, Jr., in a keynote address delivered at the Proctor Conference in 2005, looked at Isaiah 61 and at Luke 4 to point out that the Holy Spirit anoints the preacher of the Gospel (the preacher of the Good News) to address social ills, healthcare, the criminal justice system, psychological enslavement, social ills, corporate sin, individual sin and the total person. Those are the realities of this present age.

They were the reality of the present age to which Isaiah preached and they were also the realities of the present age to which Jesus preached. They are also our present realities.

The preachments that we hear today, however, do not serve this present age. They do not address those issues adumbrated by Otis Moss, Jr., illustrated by Samuel DeWitt Proctor and celebrated by Gardner C. Taylor and Miles Jerome Jones.

An African hermeneutic in the preaching of the gospel does not mean the simple cataloging or calling out in litany-like fashion the names of African men and women. It means preaching from an African-centered perspective. It means using an African-centered and pre-Columbia (indeed, pre-colonial!) starting point in terms of talking about the gospel of Jesus Christ.

An African hermeneutic in the preached word means starting from a place where there is no middle class, upper class, or lower class. The degrees that African people earn in undergraduate school, graduate school, and professional schools are simply social indicators as to how those people make a living. The church of Jesus Christ and the gospel a socially conscious minister preaches, however, has to do with how people make a *life* (not a living)!

This hermeneutic undercuts the foundation from prosperity preaching. As a matter of fact, this African-centered hermeneutic cuts the heart out of that drivel that is passing itself off as gospel when, in fact, it is nothing but the theology of Adam Smith dressed up in religious language.

An African-centered hermeneutic as the place on which the preacher stands week-after-week and the vantage point from which he or she speaks the truth in love is a hermeneutic that does not push for middle-class values or middle-income goals. It does not preach *favorites* or allow for "big Is and little yous." It does not countenance sexism, racism or heterosexism. It sees all of God's children as being simply that–*all* of God's children!

There are no stepchildren in the Kingdom of God.

Dr. Jerome Ross, Professor of Hebrew Bible, while a professor at the Samuel DeWitt Proctor School of Theology at Virginia Union University, wrote an invaluable piece in the *festschrift* for Henry Mitchell and Ella Mitchell. That volume is titled "Born to Preach".

In Dr. Ross' chapter he gives an African-centered hermeneutic that is crucial for the reading of the text, a faithful exegesis of the text and the proclamation of the text that does not do violence to what the Word of God was saying and does not do violence to what the text says to us today, in this present age!

Dr. Ross points out that not one word between Genesis 1 and Genesis 22 was written by a people who were not under oppression! Every word in our Bible was written by a people under oppression. They were under one of six different kinds of oppression as they wrote every word that we cherish and hold dear as the sacred text that informs our faith.

They were under Egyptian oppression, Assyrian oppression, Babylonian oppression, Persian oppression, Greek oppression, and Roman oppression, and they were under those oppressions from Genesis 1 all the way through Revelation 22!

Not turning our backs on Africa and serving this present age means reading those texts through the lenses of a people who understand what it means to be oppressed, a people for whom "life ain't been no crystal stair," and it also means preaching faithfully to Africans living in Diaspora. It means preaching a word of hope and a word of heritage.

Their African heritage will no longer let them turn their back on their home. Their hope is in Christ Jesus through whom we can do all things–even reclaim and redeem the Continent that was dehumanized, demonized and destroyed by white supremacy, white supremacists philosophy, white supremacists theology, and outright greed!

The preparation for the act of preaching the gospel week-after-week should take this African-centered hermeneutic into consideration. The preaching of the gospel should use the finest paradigms established for us by the black women who are preaching giants and the black men who have taught us how to *tell the story*.

The sermons preached each week from the black pulpit should lead into a prophetic practice of ministry, so that the African American believer in this present age can move from just having church to *being* the church long after the benediction has been given in his or her church.

Worship is key to Africans. Worship is key to the life of all believers and worship is key to the life of all healthy congregations in the African American tradition. Work is crucial, but work flows out of vibrant worship!

If our worship is to remain vibrant, meaningful, and have integrity, I submit to you that we need to take Gardner Taylor's challenge seriously and not turn our back on our Motherland while serving *this present age* under the anointing of him who is Lord throughout every age!

Sincerely and respectfully yours,
Pastor Jeremiah A. Wright, Jr.

Notes

[1] Charles Wesley, "A Charge to Keep I Have" (Stanza 2) 1762.

Afrocentric Theology for the Black Church

SAFIYAH FOSUA

'Friend, lend me three loaves of bread; for a friend of mine has arrived, and I have nothing to set before him' (Luke 11:5–6 NRSV).

My personal love affair with the Bible was rekindled on my first trip to Africa. My husband Kwasi and I took that long first trip together from Iowa to New York City to Amsterdam to Accra. Most international flights arrive in Ghana at night. We arrived well into the evening and it was a long time from climbing down the stairs of the plane, to retrieving our luggage, to going through customs to finally breathing the outside air. We arrived at the hotel somewhere between 11 p.m. and midnight, disoriented, out of sync from the time zone changes, and hungry! Old instincts told us to look for a vending machine because the hotel's restaurant was closed. But, there were no vending machines, and besides that we had no Ghanaian money. The street vendors were still out, so we went looking for food. When it looked as if all the food was home-cooked, we decided that wasn't our best introduction to the food of a new country. So, it was back to the hotel to ask for snacks in the bar. It was then that someone led us into an empty dining room and said, "Sit here." Shortly, another woman passed through the dining room and told us to wait. That woman set places for us at the table and within half an hour returned with two freshly-cooked fish dinners. They had awakened the cook to take care of our needs! When we bowed our heads to pray over our first meal on the Continent, we salted the food with our tears and gave thanks for hearing and seeing the Bible in action. Two years later, we returned to Ghana as missionaries. The American church called us missionaries because we worked abroad, but when people asked us where we were going, we simply said that we were needed at home.

> *'Friend, lend me three loaves of bread; for a friend of mine has arrived, and I have nothing to set before him.'*

As I said from the beginning, living in Ghana rekindled my love affair with the Bible. I thought of all the sermons I had preached before that time–many of them in cross-cultural situations. I thought of all the time, sermon time, I spent making sure people in America understood ancient biblical customs. But in Ghana, the gospel needed no translation. People in the culture understood that if a person came to visit you, even if it was just to deliver a message, you entered into no conversation whatsoever until you stopped to give them a cool drink of water. There was a sense of protocol about each visit. First, you offered cool water. If the person was dusty or dry, you refreshed him or her. Then, you get down to the reason for the visit. "Why are you here?" Time and time again, I had to stop myself from rushing to the business before caring for the person.

Remember Jesus' words at the home of Simon the Pharisee:

> *Then turning toward the woman, he said to Simon, "Do you see this woman? I entered your house; you gave me no water for my feet, but she has bathed my feet with her tears and dried them with her hair. You gave me no kiss, but from the time I came in she has not stopped kissing my feet. You did not anoint my head with oil, but she has anointed my feet with ointment" (Luke 7:44-46 NRSV).*

In Ghana, I fell in love with the Bible all over again; and it was in Ghana that I fell in love with being Black all over again. I could see and recognize myself, my aunts my uncles, my family in the faces of those I met. It was there I was able to affirm what Joseph Murphy said in his book *Working the Spirit*[1]– no matter where you put us and no matter what religion we say we practice, there is something distinctly and identifiably African about us that overrides all other things. This *something* is the reason why black Baptists don't really sound that different from black Presbyterians, black Methodists black Lutherans, black Episcopalians or even some black Catholics! That is why you may experience the presence of God in familiar ways in any of those places or why you might hear the same familiar phrases in any place where black people worship. People of African descent are stamped with a wonderfully peculiar cultural stamp that is recognizable. We come from a place where the gospel needs little or no translation. Why? I propose it is because we come from the world where the Bible was written.

In *How African Religion Changed the American Church*, Rev. Willie Wilson refers to recent discoveries about the Lemba people of South Africa, people who attracted the attention of Newsweek magazine in 1999. Why? Because scientists proved genetically through DNA testing these African people were also Jewish! Lemba men had the *Cohen gene*–a genetic variation known to occur only in those believed to be descendants of Aaron's priesthood from the Old Testament. For hundreds of years these people had said they once lived in Judea. For hundreds of years Lemba people had been telling folks they had migrated from Jerusalem but no one believed them because they were black! Further study revealed that fifty-three percent of the men of one particular clan of the Lemba people had the Cohen gene, compared to forty-five percent of Ashkenazi Jewish priests and fifty-six percent of Sephardic Jewish priests.[2] Add to this, the Lemba people observe several Jewish customs; they circumcise their boy babies on the eighth day and slaughter their animals like rabbis do in Jewish communities today. And, they are not the only black Jews, just a group unknown until 1999. In 1977 black Jews from Ethiopia were airlifted into Israel because no one could dispute that they were descendents of the twelve tribes of Israel.[3]

Where did they come from? In 1 Kings 10 we hear how the Queen of Sheba visited Solomon and learned firsthand about his grandeur. We know she was a black queen because Sheba was one of Cush's sons, descendents of Ham. This powerful African queen spent time with Solomon (the same Solomon who had 300 wives and 700 additional women on the side). While there, Ethiopians will tell you she became pregnant and that the son of that union was named Menelek. When Menelek was old enough to travel, his mother took him to see his father, Solomon, who sent a rabbi home with him so he could properly learn his father's faith–Jewish practices that continue until this day.

Let us step back a few more centuries into biblical history and look at the table of the nations. Some commonly believe that Noah's son, Ham, was a black man. His sons were Cush, Mizraim (Egypt), Phut (Libya), and Canaan. Their descendents became the Hittites, the Ninevites, the Hivites, the Girgashites, etc.

We already know Hagar was an Egyptian (son of Mizraim–a son of Ham), and that Moses married Zipporah a Cushite.[4] Rahab was a Canaanite–a woman of Jericho in the land of Canaan (another son of Ham). Bathsheba married Uriah the Hittite[5] (Hittites were also descendents of Canaan–a son of Ham).

Why is this genealogy important? Ask Matthew:

> *. . . and Aram the father of Aminadab, and Aminadab the father of Nahshon, and Nahshon the father of Salmon, and Salmon the father of Boaz by Rahab, and Boaz the father of Obed by Ruth, and Obed the father of Jesse, and Jesse the father of King David. And David was the father of Solomon by the wife of Uriah, and Solomon the father of Rehoboam, and Rehoboam the father of Abijah, and Abijah the father of Asaph (Matthew 1:4–7 NRSV).*

> *. . . and Eliud the father of Eleazar, and Eleazar the father of Matthan, and Matthan the father of Jacob, and Jacob the father of Joseph the husband of Mary, of whom Jesus was born, who is called the Messiah (Matthew 1:15–16 NRSV).*

If we are to accept the Bible account, this means that some of Ham's descendents were in King David's genealogy and subsequently in the family line of Christ! If Blacks are so profoundly represented in the Bible, then why are we so timid about statements like *unashamedly black and unapologetically Christian* (the motto of Trinity United Church of Christ in Chicago, Illinois)? I would suggest it is because, as part of the minority population of the United States, we are caught in the dualistic trap W.E.B. Dubois described:

> After the Egyptian and Indian, the Greek and Roman, the Teuton and Mongolian, the Negro is a sort of seventh son, born with a veil, and gifted with second sight in this American world,–a world which yields him no true self-consciousness, but only lets him see himself through the revelation of the other world. It is a peculiar sensation, this double-consciousness, this sense of always looking at one's self through the eyes of others, of measuring one's soul by the tape of a world that looks on in amused contempt and pity. One ever feels his twoness,–an American, a Negro; two souls, two thoughts, two unreconciled strivings; two warring ideals in one dark body, whose dogged strength alone keeps it from being torn asunder. The history of the American Negro is the history of this strife,–this longing to attain self-conscious manhood, to merge his double self into a better and truer self. . . .[6]

What is the way forward? The late Robert Webber, of the Ancient-Future series, said that the "road to the future runs through the past." The need to understand and embrace an African past is the strength of the story of Sankofa. Ghanaians tell the legend of the Sankofa bird this way:

> There was once a bird, a not so smart bird, known for laying her eggs, then walking off and leaving them behind. Other animals noticed this bird was so stupid that she kept leaving her eggs unattended. Finally, they stopped her and said: "Eh! Look behind you; you are leaving something! You better go back and fetch it!"

That is why images of the Sankofa bird have her head turned backward and there is often an egg in the picture. Hence the words in Akan: San–*turn*; Ko–*go*; Fa–*pick it up!* If that dumb bird didn't invest time in hatching her eggs, there would be no more birds like her. If we do not invest time in passing our values on to the next generation and the one after that, they will truly be lost. We have left our eggs often to hatch on their own while we chased the American dream and we wonder what has happened. This present generation is the first generation of young people to completely shun the Church. Hip-hop music is the first musical form coming from black folks that does not have roots of some kind in the black church. And yet in their stumbling in the dark, I see this generation trying to go back and fetch it for us. A recent HBO documentary reminded us that street gangs began with young men banded together for the good of the community.[7] Gangs continue because of the sense of community, though misguided. They do so at a time the church is no longer the center of the community.

David LaChappelle produced a documentary on the Krump dance phenomena[8] that has begun to overshadow gangs in parts of Southern California. In his documentary, we learn clown-dance groups function as communities that give their members identity, and thanks to the miracles of technology, viewers see comparisons of krump dancing's movements with certain traditional dance moves from the African continent. Again, it looks like young people are looking for what we left behind.

Sankofa. Turn, GO BACK, and PICK it UP. What do we find that we want to bring forward? Dr. Lamin Sanneh, a native of Gambia who teaches at Yale University, brought an interesting concept into the conversation in his book, *Whose Religion is Christianity: the Gospel beyond the West* (2003, Eerdmans). He speaks of the indigenous discovery of Christianity rather than Christian discovery of indigenous societies.[9] While his claim may sound like an exercise in semantics, the implications are huge. When we look only at indigenous (meaning cultural or contextual) expressions of the Christian faith, it is easy to focus all our attention on how people take the version of Christianity that we offer to them and make it theirs. Look at how they take our songs and give them new tunes! Look at how they take our ideas and make them more palatable for their own communities! If we only look at indigenous societies within the larger framework of established Christianity we are tempted to focus our attention on lyrics and art forms, hip-hop dancers and organists–while missing more important aspects of faith, like beliefs and faith practices. But, if we shift our attention as Sanneh encourages us to do, we are forced to consider how indigenous people *find the faith.*

What did people who were indigenous to Africa find in Christianity that perhaps had been overlooked even by their captors? We know what they were offered. Historical journals are filled with accounts of how slavers used Christianity to calm rebellious slaves down. They were given *slaves obey your masters* in Ephesians and Colossians. They were handed *slaves submit to your masters in all things–even when they are harsh* in Peter. They were spoon-fed *slaves don't talk back to your masters* in Titus. They were given a distorted view of gospel and Christ. Instead of hearing that the *Spirit of the Lord was upon the Church to free the oppressed*, their oppression was justified.

In the 1970s when Roots was first released on American TV, I was living in West Germany. The series was not available on German TV, so those of us who wanted to see it went together to a military base theatre to view it as a movie, three episodes per night. For those of you who watched it night after night or week after week, you remember the pain and the anger that erupted. Imagine *three* episodes in one night. I remember sitting in the movie theater that first night hurt and stunned, surrounded by strangers. Behind me, a mother had brought her little girl who was understandably distraught by what she saw. At intermission, this tearful little girl asked her mother, "Mama why were they so mean to those people?" When her mother answered, "Honey I know it was awful, but that was what it took for those people to receive Christianity . . . " there was nearly a riot in the theater that night!

We know from many accounts the slaves were not given a liberating gospel; instead the Bible was used as a tool of subjugation. On the positive side, what happens when indigenous people *discover* Christianity? What happens when slaves, forbidden to read, secretly are taught and secretly teach each other? What happens when slaves hear the call to preach? I'll tell you what happens. We start hearing a hermeneutic of suspicion in lyrics like "everybody talking bout heaven ain't going there!" We start hearing a theology of equality in lyrics like "didn't my Lord deliver Daniel?" We start hearing strains of liberation theology in "Wade in the water, wade in the water children, God's gonna trouble the water!" We begin to see people willing to give their very lives to s h a k e off the shackles of injustice.

I do not believe that this kind of liberation only happens once in a people's history. Nor do I believe the process is reserved for marginalized people. What was it about Quakers that enabled them to discovery Christianity differently from their neighbors? What was it about those who hosted Underground Railroad stations in their homes or churches; what did they discover in Christianity? What was it about a young man named Martin, a young adult, named after his daddy, holding a prestigious young adult office in his national church who dared to risk it all because he could not escape the words: *let justice flow like waters and righteousness like an ever-flowing stream*?

Afrocentric theology continually invites us to shift our focus to rediscovering the text and tenets of the Christian faith. It calls us to move beyond *repeat after me* . . . and *there will be a test!*–to *what is the Christian faith* and *what must I do once I find it*? If *we* could put aside, just for a minute, what we have been handed and rediscover Christianity, as people of African descent, what might we find?

Afrocentric theology helps us rediscover God's nature and Jesus' teachings. It helps us rediscover Jesus who took up time with the women and children and elevated womanhood for all time by allowing one woman to anoint him for burial with precious perfume and another to be the first to proclaim him alive. Jesus, who resisted religious leaders who were motivated by power or prestige or greed more than by a desire to bring people closer to God. Jesus, who was willing to give everything he had–even his very life to make eternal life available to us all. Jesus, *Mary's baby*, who never said a mumbling word. Jesus, who instead of pimping prosperity proclaimed that birds have nests and foxes have holes but the Son of Man had nowhere to lay his head! We might be forced to ask, in the backlight of a country taken with the prosperity gospel, what so many people in starving countries find in the gospel. Instead of filling up our own store houses we might find ourselves saying with John Wesley, "*Give all you can, do all you can, as long as you can to as many people as you can!*"

When we rediscover the text, especially through the eyes of the African community, the village, we will rediscover the Old Testament principle that God made enough of everything for the world, but it is distributed wrongly. We will remember it is wrong to say or act out *I got mine and you got yours to get!* Instead, New Testament writers remind us that faith without works is dead.

We thank James Cone for placing black theology on the map in his landmark work, *For My People* and *God of the Oppressed*[10]. Cone is credited with laying the foundations to understand what we have always lived and preached, a gospel of liberation. We embraced the stories of the Exodus and looked closely (non-readers and readers alike) at the Bible stories of deliverance from terrible situations. It would have been so easy to turn away from the God of our oppressors and run back to the gods we left behind but we stumbled across the words: *he was wounded for our transgressions* and identified personally with Jesus of the gospels.

Henry Mitchell, the godfather of black preaching, dignified black preaching–the same preaching that had been labeled excessive and too emotive–by talking about the transformative nature of preaching in the black community. In our community, preaching is not simple exposition; it is an encounter between God and people where the people are both healed and empowered. Mitchell, in his landmark book *Soul Theology*[11], shows us how to identify theology in the folk wisdom of the elders. For example, people in the community speak frequently of God's omnipotence: *He is so high; you can't git over him . . . so wide you can't get around him* . . . . And, people speak about God's justice on street corners and porches across the land when old folks say: *You gonna reap just what you sow.*

Dwight Hopkins, in *Shoes that Fit our Feet*[12], points out illustrations are to be found within our own culture. We do not always need pore through *Chicken Soup for the Soul* looking for sermon illustrations; they may be readily found in sources like the slave and liberation narratives, the spirituals, Brer' Rabbit stories, or even Toni Morrison novels! Hopkins shows us how everyday illustrations that highlight gospel truths are found among us because we are a people who have historically worked to live the faith, even in political arenas.

Twenty-first century biblical scholars like Brian Blount and Randall Bailey give us ways to approach texts consistent with ways black people think about the faith, with the end result of empowering worshippers to walk in the faith with integrity and with confidence. Scholars like Barbara Holmes, author of *Joy Unspeakable*[13], remind us we are not latecomers to spiritual disciplines or to the spiritual formation movement; we have always been part of spiritual formation traditions. In fact, many of our worship gatherings are contemplation in community.

Afrocentric theology is not a cry for black supremacy or to dwell upon an unpleasant task; it is a call to worship and think about God with our eyes, ears, and hearts open. It calls us to wear our own eyeglasses and live in our own skin–yes even to speak with our own voice as we rediscover the Christ of dusty roads and the God of the Old Testament. Afrocentric theology affords us an opportunity to proclaim how we human beings are created in the image of God; how we have strayed from that image and have broken God's heart. Finally, Afrocentric theology affords us an opportunity to reconnect with worshippers in the black church. In a church environment where seminary is not so teasingly called *cemetery* and where whole denominations are anti-education, Afrocentric theology reminds us Jesus made his weighty words accessible through wisdom forms. He spoke in parables, used agricultural examples, and spoke to the needs and issues of the people who were present. One modern-day criticism of the church is that it continues to preach about the sins of the 1950s while ignoring new problems that have arisen today. For example, when was the last time you heard anything from the pulpit about crystal meth? How often do you hear that heterosexual black women who are faithful to their spouses or boyfriends are now the largest group contracting HIV/AIDS?

Virginia Union Seminary professor John Kinney told our DMin class at United Theological Seminary about his first pastoral appointment. He was fresh out of seminary and eager to please, or should I say dazzle, people who had followed his academic career. So, his first sermons were homiletically perfect! He used every big word he knew and explained every theological concept he had learned, and even managed to say a couple of words about the text. At the end of his sermon he was quite proud of himself. "My professors would be pleased," he thought. He rushed to the door to shake hands with people as they left the building. Straggling from the building was an old woman. You know her. She moves a little slow. Her wig is a bit outdated. But she speaks the truth in love. This old saint came to shake the preacher's hand and said this to him: "Son, you've done real well in school and we're so proud of you–but if you don't mind, would you please bring me my water in a cup I recognize!" Needless to say, Professor Kinney recognized that what he had done was not at all helping his congregation.

Afrocentric theology invites us to remember who we are. It invites us to remember the people to whom and with whom we are in ministry. It invites us to worship with our eyes open, to see human need, and to remember God's nature and Jesus Christ's mission. Afrocentric theology invites us to keep it real and keep it relevant!

I end where I started: *Friend, can you lend me three loaves, for a friend of mine has just come in from out of town and I have nothing to set before him.* When someone calls upon you to break the bread of life in the black church, make sure the bread was baked in your own oven. Amen.

Notes

[1] Joseph M. Murphy, *Working the Spirit: Ceremonies of the African Diaspora* (Boston, MA: Beacon Press, 1995).

[2] Reverend Willie Wilson, *How African Religion Changed the American Church*, Copyright 2004, Reverend Willie Wilson

[3] The History of Ethiopian Jews" from the Jewish Virtual Library http://www.jewishvirtuallibrary.org/jsource/Judaism/ejhist.html
[4] Numbers 12:1
[5] 2 Samuel 11:3
[6] Excerpted from the chapter "Of Our Spiritual Strivings" in his book *The Souls of Black Folk.*
http://www.duboislc.org/html/DoubleConsciousness.html
[7] HBO documentary "Bastards of the Party," (2005) directed by Antoine Fuqua (Training Day), takes its name from a phrase in Mike Davis' history of Los Angeles and traces the beginnings of the most notorious street gangs in Los Angeles. This documentary was acclaimed best documentary at the 2005 American Black Film Festival, the 2006 Hollywood Black Film Festival and the 2006 International Black Cinema Festival.
[8] "Rize" documentary directed by David LaChappelle (2005).
[9] Lamin Sanneh, *Whose Religion is Christianity: The Gospel beyond the West* (Grand Rapids, MI: Eerdman 2003), 10.
[10] James Cone, *God of the Oppressed* (Maryknoll, NY: Orbis, 1997). This book has been reprinted many times. It was originally published in 1975.
[11] Henry Mitchell and Nicholas Cooper-Lewter, *Soul Theology, The Heart of American Black Culture* (Nashville, TN: Abingdon, 1991).
[12] Dwight N. Hopkins, *Shoes that Fit our Feet: Sources for a Constructive Black Theology* (Maryknoll, NY: Orbis, 1993).
[13] Barbara A. Holmes, *Joy Unspeakable: Contemplative Practices of the Black Church* (Minneapolis, MN: Augsburg Fortress, 2004).

Worshipping Contextually: Bassa People in the United Methodist Church in Liberia

PIANAPUE KEPT EARLY

One strong component of worship in Bassa United Methodist Churches in Liberia is the choir. The choir helps to hold the worship experience together and augments the pastor's message through the use of songs and through its participation in the ministries of the church. Choirs use several kinds of songs or music traditions in the St. John River District, a predominantly Bassa ethnic district of the UMC in Liberia. The two most common forms of music are the traditional Bassa church songs and hymns translated from the United Methodist and the Baptist hymnals.

In order to understand the importance of the choir in the Bassa-speaking churches of the Church in Liberia, it is important to describe the basic structure of the choir. Each choir has a leader: a man or woman, who directs the workings of the group. He or she sometimes serves as "President" in situations where bureaucracy is important. In addition, there is the Choir Matron, often an elderly woman, whose selection is based upon her level of participation in the choir, her dedication and commitment, as well as her ability. Some matrons are selected solely for their dedication, regardless of their age. Besides the President and Choir Matron, there may be alto, tenor, soprano, and bass section leaders. Choir members are assigned to the respective voice groups.

The Bassa church choir brings a cultural as well as a spiritual flavor to the service. The traditional Bassa church songs have many unique characteristics. Traditional Bassa church songs are usually sung in harmony and accompanied by drums, tambourines, and in rare cases, western musical instruments. Most of the traditional church songs are done in the *call-and-response* manner. One person starts the song, then another person repeats the line, and *then* the choir and the congregation join in. If the congregation does not already know the song, before the song ends, some people will have learned it just from listening. If at the next service that particular song is sung, the entire congregation is usually able to sing along. This is what one Bassa scholar[1] refers to as "responsive singing".

Bassa Methodist Christians use songs from the UMC hymnal because this helps to continue the musical tradition of the Methodist Church, which started with John and his brother Charles Wesley. I add here that the translation of hymns is not unique to the Bassa churches alone. The Kru, Grebo, and Kpelle Christians also translate hymns in their native languages. Bassa translators realize that sometimes, for rhythmic structure and coherence, it is not always possible for every word in English to correspond to a word in Bassa. As such, translation then becomes a form of interpretation. The Bassa New Testament translation called *De Wudu Die*, contains passages which one can read with connotations different from the English translations of the Greek expressions.

Here are examples of two familiar worship offerings translations into Bassa. One is the song, "Blessed Assurance, Jesus is Mine," and the other is the Apostle's Creed. Both translations vary slightly in meaning from the original English versions, but maintain their significance in Christianity.

***Mna Whodo Kon De Wudu* (In Bassa)–**
Blessed Assurance (English)

Mna whodo kon de wudu, Poinyon mon ni nyon
Blessed assurance, (the) Savior is mine
O fuanfuan deh ah dyea, mua deh dah gahn;
O What a foretaste of Glory divine
Ne orh mon poin-kpe, Poinyon dah toh
Then it is a saving power, the Savior has given
Wodo de orh zuuor mu, deede de orh numun mu.
Born of the Spirit, bathed in his blood.

Chorus :
Dea ke mon non-wudu, dea ke mon wede,
This is a story, this is a song
Be ah ke Poinyon bahn, de we seyn xweden
That we can praise the Savior, all the day long
Dea ke mon non-wudu, dea ke mon wede,
This is a story, this is a song
Be ah ke Poinyon bahn, de we seyn xweden
That we can praise the Savior, all the day long.

***'Postle Creed" (In Bassa)* The Apostle's Creed (In English)**
Um po Gedeporh-Vene je jai, Gedeporh-vene mon ah ba
I believe in the Almighty God. The Almighty is our Father
Orh nyun dyun, ke orh nyun bede. Um poeh jai, orh toei dyu
He is the maker of Heaven and the earth. I believe He sent his son
Jize. Jize dyen zuu-vene. Orh wodo voijae Maide xwheden,
Jesus. Jesus was conceived through the Big Spirit.
Born of the Virgin Mary
orh dye gah, orh meyn Kahn Padi dyua, wah za dyodeen,
He suffered, he died in the presence of King Pilate. He was buried
orh nyun giohn wey-sohn, weyor-tahn ne nyen, orh wodoe de.
He spent two days in death, and rose on the third day
Orh mu dyuen, de Gedeporh dea-sohn kon,
He went up to Heaven, on the right hand side of God
De-orh ne kayn, bo-ah be.
That's where he is now, on our behalf.
Um poeh jai, de Gedeporn dea-sohn kon, ne,
I believe truthfully, that from that right hand side of God
De orh ke swein, jeleme wauy teyn, orh ke bodo torh kpa yee.
He will come again, on the day of Judgment, to serve as lawyer
for the world
Um poeh jai, Gedeporh nyon zuu vene je
I believe truthfully, the Holy Spirit of God's people
Um poeh jai, Gedeporh nyon dorh dede,
I believe truthfully, the conversations of God's people
Nyon namman kwein zein-zein, kpodo-dyua dye sor-sor,
The forgiveness of our sins, the resurrection of the body
Bo sey-naisian ti mu, – Ka orh menee.
For life everlasting, let it be so.

The translation of the two texts above, as you have noticed, is not exactly as stated in the English versions used by the Church. This is a unique form of translation that, in Bassa Churches, speaks to the context. For example, in the song, "Blessed Assurance," the expression, "Heir of Salvation, purchased of God," does not have a direct translation in this sense, and so, the Bassa saying, "Then it is a saving power, given by God," substitutes for the original expression. This gives the hymn a slightly different meaning, while it maintains the tune of the song. I have seen missionaries who visit the Bassa Churches sing along even though what they were singing in English was not an exact translation. While we Bassa Christians may read the Apostle's Creed in our context, our understanding of the Creed does not contradict or conflict what is written in English. The main difference in both versions is the expression or emphasis, and the significance we assign to certain concepts. The contextual readings help us worship God fully, in Spirit and in Truth.

Bibliography

Early, J. Cephas. *The United Methodist Church among the Bassa People in Liberia: Personal Memoirs of Rev. J. Cephas Early, Sr.* Atlanta, Georgia: 1998 (Unpublished Manuscript).

Karnga, Abba. *ABBA: God's Warrior in Liberia.* Pasadena, California: World Wide Missions, 1994.

__________. *My People, the Bassa Tribe.* Pasadena, California: World Wide Missions, 1975.

__________. "Political, Theological and Missological Development among the Bassa in Liberia," in African Independent Churches. David Shank, (Ed). Elkhart, Indiana: Mennonite Board of Missions, 1991.

Pichl, W. J. "L'Ecriture Bassa au Liberia." Bulletin de l'IFAN T XXVIII, Ser. B, No. 1-2. 1966), 480-484.

Scheffers, Mark. "Schism in the Bassa Independent Churches of Liberia," Unpublished Manuscript.

Shank, David (Ed.). *Ministry in Partnership with African Independent Churches.* Elkhart, Indiana: Mennonite Board of Missions, 1991.

Siegmann, William. *Ethnographic Survey of Southeastern Liberia: Report on the Bassa.* Robertsport, Liberia: Tubman Center of African Culture, 1969.

Tinklinberg, Perry. *Christian Extension Ministries of the CEFL.* Buchanan, Liberia: CEFL Production Center, n.d.

Vanderra, Larry. *The Bassa of Liberia: A Study of Culture, Historical Development and Indigenization of the Gospel.* Deerfield, Illinois, 1982.

Notes

[1] Joseph M. N. Gbadyu, a Bassa leader, made this observation on the Christian radio station in Liberia, ELWA in 1974.

Translatability as Belonging: Bassa United Methodist Christians in Liberia

PIANAPUE KEPT EARLY

Since the nineteenth century, missionaries to Africa have adopted the policy of translating the Bible (translated first into English from the Aramaic, Hebrew, and Greek), into the local languages of various African peoples. This *translatability*–the act of translating the Bible and other Christian literature into the local language, in this case, Bassa–is one practice that benefits the Bassa people of Liberia on their Christian journey. Christian missionaries among the Bassa, William Crocker,[1] June Hobley,[2] Don Slager,[3] Mark Schleffers,[4] among others, felt it would be easier to witness to Bassa people and win more souls for Christ by translating portions of the Bible or the entire Bible into the Bassa language. These translation helped missionaries to reach Bassa people with the Christian message. The translations also helped Bassa Christians to feel like the Christian faith belongs to them. This short essay describes what this belongingness means to Bassa Christians.

Bassa People in Liberia

Bassa People in Liberia are among the oldest surviving ethnic population in Liberia. Bassa people are part of the Kwa (or Kru) linguistic group[5] which incorporates other coastal and interior peoples, including the Belle, Dey, Grebo, Krahn, and Kru Peoples. The Kwa are primarily coastal peoples. Their sociopolitical structure is decentralized, resulting in smaller villages, towns, or enclaves. By contrast, the Liberian Government in their quest to conquer the interior peoples and incorporate them into the political mainstream encouraged the Kwa to create clans, towns, and paramount chiefs. Compared to the other two major linguistic groups, the Mel and the Mande[6], the Kwa have smaller towns, villages, or enclaves. Bassa people live life to its fullest, with less material and more of the spirit. Bassa are artisans: wordsmiths, musicians, entertainers, farmers, diviners, black smiths, and smelters.

The name "Bassa' represents the land, language, and the people. The name for the people was originally "*NaO nyon*" [people who say]. The other name was "*Gbo-nyon*," a synonym of *NaO nyon*. This name was later changed when a Chief, whose nickname was "Rock", because of his warring strength, ensured that none of his subjects were sent or sold to slavery. As a result, each time he traveled, a large entourage followed him, to protect him as well as themselves. And when other people saw them coming, they would say, "Father [*Ba Sorh, literally, Father Rock*] and his people are coming." The name "Bassa" came to represent this Chief and his people, and they have since dropped the name, *NaO- nyon*, and adopted the Bassa as their official name.[7]

Approximately one million Bassa people live in Liberia and in exile. Bassa counties[8] include, Grand Bassa, Rivercess, Margibi, and Montserrado. Bassa people also have communities in the other counties.[9] Each of the Bassa counties, with the exception of Margibi, lies along the coast of the Atlantic Ocean, and the Bassa homeland extends northeast up to 350 miles into the interior of Liberia.

Grand Bassa County divides evenly between mountains and lowlands. Bassa County has many hills and mountains. Karnga describes Bassa land by identifying the following mountain ranges: *Jui,* or Findley Mountain Range; *Goh-Tro* Range; *Seayah* Range; *Dyahnford* Range; *Seehngbah-Tro* Range; *Doe [Dooh]* Range; and *Baah-Tro* Range.[10] The Jui, or Findley Mountain Range extends along the *Dabahn* (St. John) River, from Nimba County to Buchanan City.

Bassa County has numerous rivers, creeks, falls, and brooks flowing from the mountains. The famous rivers are *Dabahn* (the St. John) River, which is the largest. Others include *Nibnuehn,* or Rivercess, (Cestos River); *Bioh,* or Timbo

River; *Yahn,* or Newcess River; *Diahn,* or Farmington River; Zlor River; *Gbii* River; *Wii* River; *Duahn* River; Benson River; and *Doahn* River.[11] At least five of these rivers[12] collect water from other smaller streams and empty into the Atlantic. Liberia's tropical climate produces rainy and dry seasons. Farming season in Bassa land extends from January through May, sometimes lasting through October. The months of July through September are heavier rainy months.

Bassa people see themselves in four different family groups: *Gboo, Geegbahn, Gbahngbon,* and *Swah.* The group one identifies with determines the taboos, totems, and norms a person lives by. The *Gboo* family group should never consume or eat dogs, *dyui,* or the ricebird; palm wine, palm cabbage, and thorny cabbage. *Geegbahn* or *Munn* family should never consume or eat goat and monkey. The *Gbahngbon* or *Nyehnkpor* family should never consume or eat fresh water fish. They may "hate the fish, but they drink the water which produces the fish." The fourth family group, *Swah* or *Garn,* should not consume leopards, opossums, or snakes of any kind. It is fair to say that Bassa people family network is like a spider's web, connected to a primary source, *Bah Sorh.* It is unclear if Bassa people in the cities maintain strong family group identity because of influences like the Christian family model and western education.

Karnga observes that "animism, transmigration, and herbalism" define Bassa supernatural beliefs.[13] Bassa people believed in some supreme being before Christianity dominated. Diviners or Herbalists, sometimes called medicine men or women, teach the beliefs. Bassa diviners fall into two groups: the "*Hwiohn*" and "*Hwe-nyon*" depending on how each performs. The *Hwion* is the diviner who uses herbs to heal the sick and afflicted. The *Hwe-nyon* is the diviner who uses herbs to do evil or harm. While people see the former diviner as generally good, they see the latter as wicked, fearful, and therefore evil.

As stated previously, Bassa culture is not stagnant because of its encounters with the wider world. Like other people, Bassa culture is adjusting to realities of the twenty-first century world. What impact does Christianity make on Bassa people's lives?

Bassa Methodist Christians see translatability as a sign of belonging to the Church–counteracting any notion that the Church was not originally meant for them. Having a portion of the Bible and some of the hymns translated into Bassa offers Bassa Christians a new prism through which to view themselves as part of God's chosen people. Christianity has exposed Bassa people to a new way of perceiving the world, not as a closed circle, but as an open space where all God's children can relate, interact, and worship God in spirit and in truth.

Every Sunday, in Bassa-speaking United Methodist Church congregations, Bassa-speaking ministers and pastors preach from the Bible, portions of which are translated to the native Bassa language. The choir sings hymns from the UMC hymnal, translated into Bassa. The congregation recites the Lord's Prayer, the Apostle's Creed, and the Psalm 23 in Bassa, as part of the liturgy. The responsive readings get a Bassa response.

English-speaking visitors, especially visiting missionaries, government officials, and other professional persons, feel at home because the service is conducted in both Bassa and English. They can participate in the worship service by responding to the responsive reading, singing, and reciting the creeds. Some of the many passages from the Bible that ministers or preachers will often use are Matthew 28:19; Mark 16:1–8; Luke 19:2ff., and John 3:16ff. Songs one will likely hear include, "Blessed Assurance," "How Great Thou Art," "What a Friend We Have in Jesus," "My Faith Looks Up to Thee," and "Pass Me Not O Gentle Savior," among others.

This belongingness becomes more important in light of the historic struggles of the Bassa Methodists. While the missionaries were in some ways helpful, they also imposed their culture as Christianity, destroying or describing Bassa people's culture as evil, satanic, and devilish. This was followed, in the 1940s, by tense relations with their brothers and sisters[14] of the church, versed in Western lifestyles, who ignored them, overlooked them, and insulted them. Both of these factors encouraged Bassa Christians to choose context and culture as keys of hermeneutics. Belongingness to Bassa United Methodist Christians means relating to God in their own context–a concept important for many other non-Western Christians.

The use of local translations allows for the interpretation and understanding of scripture, theology, liturgy, ecclesiology, and Christology, using local Bassa lenses. It allows for exploring God through the Bassa people's experiences and realities. Through the use of local translations Bassa Christians can better grasp contextual concepts, ideas, philosophies–God is good; Christ rose from the dead; Christ heals; or God is love–to apply a pragmatic outlook on scripture. It helps, for example, for the people to be able look to the Bible and recognize its power when they refer to the scriptures for specific healing purposes, or to address economic issues. For any Bassa man or woman who is a Christian, these are benefits of translatability.

Local translations also encourage Bassa United Methodist Christians to grow in faith by studying the Word of God for themselves. Studying the Bible as translated locally helped to decentralize numerous Bassa Christian churches. By decentralization, I mean that there are more Bassa Independent Churches, which are an outgrowth of the Mainline Denominations, like the Methodists, Baptists, or Episcopalians. The proliferation of Bassa Churches reflects a commitment to seeking truth, justice, and equity. It also demonstrates spiritual strength and the desire for a liberated approach to the Christian faith. Once people started reading the Bible (the Gospels) in their own native language, and singing the church hymns in their own tongue, they were able to dwell "under their own vine and fig tree." Bassa people in the United Methodist Church in particular, have, through this broad interest in translatability, made the church, a place of their own.

Bibliography

Bevans, Stephen B. *Models of Contextual Theology*. Maryknoll, New York: Orbis Books, 1992.

Cox, Gresham S. *Remains of Melville B. Cox, Late Missionary to Liberia* (New York: T. Mason and G. Lane, 1839), 74-98.

Early, Sr., Rev. J. Cephas. *The Story of United Methodism in Liberia: Personal Memoir of Rev. J. Cephas Early*, Sr. Atlanta, Georgia: 1998 (Unpublished Manuscript).

Forkay, Solomon. "Bassa Vah Script & History of CEFL (Christian Educational Foundation of Liberia)," Unpublished Manuscript, 1990.

Franklin, D. Bruce. "The White Methodist Image of the American Negro Emigrant to Liberia, West Africa, 1833–1848," in Methodist History, XV, # 3, (1977), 147-66.

Greenberg, Joseph. *Languages of Africa*. Bloomington, Indiana: Indiana University Press, 1966.

Greene, Graham. *Journey Without Maps*. (New York, New York: Penguin Books), 1984.

Kaliombe, Patrick A. "Spirituality in the African Perspective," in Rosino Gibellini, (Ed.), Paths of African Theology. (Maryknoll, New York: Orbis Books, 1994), 115-35.

Karnga, Abba. *ABBA: God's Warrior in Liberia*. Pasadena, California: World Wide Missions, 1974.

_______*My People, The Bassa Tribe*. Pasadena, California: World Wide Missions, 1975.

_______"Political, Theological and Missiological Development among the Bassa of Liberia," in David Shank (Ed.) Ministry in Partnership with African Independent Churches. (Elkhart, Indiana: Mennonite Board of Missions, 1991), 171-332.

Nassau, Rev. R. H. *Historical Sketch of the Missions in Africa, under the care of the Board of Foreign Missions of the Presbyterian Church*. Philadelphia: Woman's Foreign Missionary Society of the Presbyterian Church, 1881.

Okorocha, Cyril C. "The Search for Salvation (Ezi-Ndu): the Theological Key to Igbo Conversion to Christianity," in The Meaning of Religious Conversion in Africa. (Avebury: Gower Publishing House, 1987), 204-45.

Scheffers, Mark. "Schism in the Bassa Independent Churches of Liberia," (Unpublished Manuscript).

Shank, David (Editor). *Ministry in Partnership with African Independent Churches*. Elkhart, Indiana: Mennonite Board of Missions, 1991.

Staudenraus, Philip J. *The African Colonization Movement, 1816-1865*. New York: Columbia University Press, 1961.

Tinklenberg, Perry. "Christian Extension Ministries of the Christian Educational Foundation of Liberia." Unpublished Manuscript.

Vanderaa, Larry. *The Bassa of Liberia: a Study of Culture, Historical Development and Indigenization.* Deerfield, Illinois, 1992 (Unpublished Master Thesis).
Wilmore, Gayraud S. *Black Religion and Black Radicalism: An Interpretation of the Religious History of African Americans.* Maryknoll, New York: Orbis Books, 2003.

Notes

[1] William Crocker was probably the first Caucasian Baptist Missionary to Liberia. He worked among the Bassa People between 1832 to 1836.
[2] June Hobely, a Liberian Inland Mission missionary, worked and lived among the Bassa People, up to her death in 1989. She was killed by NPFL rebels loyal to Charles Taylor. She is famous for her work, English-Bassa, Bassa-English Dictionary.
[3] Don Slager works with Christian Educational Foundation of Liberia (CEFL), where their goal is to translate the Bible to English. A recent translated version of the Holy Bible in Bassa was published in 2005, under the guidance of Slager and others.
[4] Mark Scheffers also worked among the Bassa People as missionary from the Reformed Church in the USA.
[5] See Joseph Greenberg's classification on West African Languages.
[6] The Mande is the third cultural group of Liberia. They include the Kpelle, Vai, Gio, Mano, among others.
[7] Abba G. Karnga, *My People, the Bassa Tribe* (Pasadena, California: World Wide Missions, 1975), 7.
[8] In Liberia, a county is a political division. Each county hosts native peoples and Americo-Liberians. Native people are majority.
[9] The counties listed here are predominantly Bassa, with the exception of Montserrado, where there is more diversity, especially in Monrovia. The descriptions I mention above specifically refer to Grand Bassa County and Rivercess, not Margibi and Montserrado. There are 15 counties in Liberia.
[10] Karnga, 8.
[11] The original Bassa names of the rivers are in italics.
[12] The five rivers include: *Dabahn* (St. John), *Yahn* (Newcess), *Bioh* (Timbo), *Diahn* (Farmington), and *Nebuehn* (Rivercess).
[13] Karnga, 86.
[14] There has always existed tension between the Bassa UMC churches, until 1959. This conflict existed in an aged-old Liberian class struggle, where the Settlers (Americo-Liberians) have always felt to be above the native or original Liberians. I am currently working on a history of the church on this issue.

The Creation of an Africana Worship Ritual: Baptism in the *Shouters* of Trinidad

GENNIFER BENJAMIN BROOKS

The rituals of our religious and worship lives develop over time. The practices that are so common to our communities in the present–those that we consider the unquestioned norms of our worship–have been massaged and manipulated and adapted and accommodated to the places and times of those who came before us. And in a similar way, the worship rituals that we, in our time, have questioned are often the legacies of laments and celebrations of our ancestors in the faith. Ronald Grimes, a recognized scholar in the field of ritual study, believes that "the roots of ritual are various–human bodies, the environment, cultural traditions, social processes . . . (and that) ritual itself has no single origin."[1]

As noted in an article published in the January/February 2006 edition of *Circuit Rider*, the word ritual in the vocabulary of the mid-twentieth century, in what was then the British colony of Trinidad in the West Indies, "spoke of dark deeds in hidden and similarly dark places."[2] The hiddenness of the worship rituals of the captive people, exiled and enslaved far from mother Africa, was in direct response to the environment of slavery that had become their societal norm. When commanded to abandon their worship practices they developed instead a culture of secrecy that caused the proponents of their enslavement to think of their rituals as dark and therefore evil. The commitment and determination of these slaves to hold on to their worship roots in the uprootedness of their diasporic existence engendered fear in the hearts of the society into which the people had been transplanted. In response, laws were created that forbade anything African–especially the primitive voice of drums–to be part of their worship experiences. But these people, who had been torn from their homeland and who had survived atrocities through the Middle Passage, would not be denied their heritage. An underground African worship was their first response.

Arriving in the Caribbean as slaves for the plantations of the Portuguese, Spanish, and French colonists, mainly from the western shores of Africa, these ancestors "were religious. In fact, religion pervaded their lives."[3] Some were Muslims, but were unable to maintain and practice their beliefs due to the nature of life on the plantations. Although their religious patterns were to undergo significant changes, they remained recognizably African in structure and content. With the same strength of will that enabled their survival on the journey to the colonies, slaves learned ultimately to adapt their religious practices in order to circumvent the disapproval of slave masters.

The religion of these Africans centered around belief in a supreme god, infinitely good, the creator and source of all power, who resided in the sky, away from the people, and was "virtually inactive in human affairs. Involvement in human fortune and misfortune was the role of lesser deities and spirits."[4] In their homeland, some tribes maintained priests and temples that were dedicated to the supreme god, worshipped regularly at an altar, and made sacrifices and offerings through the priest. Others believed that their god did not need to be persuaded by sacrifices and prayers in order to act in the best interest of the people because the god had the divine quality of goodness. In Trinidad where the Yorubas of West Africa were most prevalent, they "lavished their worship on divinities such as Obatala, Ogun, Shango and Ifa, the orish-nla (gods) of the sky, iron or war, thunder or divination, respectively . . . "[5] The rituals of worship, common to all the tribes, involved a large degree of body movement.

> An important part of the worship service devoted to the 'lesser' gods consisted of an elaborate ceremonial dance in which priests, priestesses and devotees became "possessed" by the gods. The dance was done to the rhythm of drums. The gods who made their appearance at the dance were greeted with a litany of praise and with gifts in the form of sacrifices or libations.[6]

As a means of controlling the slaves, the plantocracy held to a policy of separating African tribesmen from one another. This affected the advancement of African religion. Although leadership arose within their ranks, they were not the trained priests and priestesses of the native lands. In addition, the priesthood required a commitment and dedication that slave status did not allow. As a result, rituals became corrupted due to both the lack of knowledge of these new leaders and to the influence of Catholicism, the religion of the settlers.

African religious practices, however, continued in secret since these rituals helped the slaves to endure the hardships of their lives in servitude. The plantocracy banned African religious practices seeing in them the impetus for resistance against slavery. The planters attempted to Christianize their slaves as a means of eliminating African religion, but this only resulted in the exchange of Roman Catholic saints for the erstwhile African gods. Further, some of the prayers offered at African worship ceremonies soon began to resemble the prayers of the saints offered in the Catholic mass. The result was that African rituals became Christianized and Christian rituals took on an African flavor, ultimately creating what might be termed new "Africana"[7] worship rituals. A prime example of this merger and the resulting worship ritual can be seen in the baptism ritual of a sect of Christianity in Trinidad called the *Shouters.*

The baptismal ritual of the Shouters can be traced to a time when Trinidad was under Catholic rulers. Trinidad was owned first by Spain and then by France, both Catholic countries. Under both Spanish and French rule, slaves received instruction for baptism and experienced baptism by immersion. Evangelical missionaries to the Caribbean, including Methodists, initially found their work difficult because of language and because of the missionaries' open objection to slavery. However as time progressed, the leadership of the evangelical movement shifted from ordained priests to educated laypersons, including freed slaves. These new leaders contributed directly to the change in the tenor of baptismal services. Soon the aura of mysticism that was part of African worship began to infiltrate the baptism service.

The baptismal ritual of Roman Catholicism practiced in this Caribbean colony included many elements of the initiation rituals of the Early Church[8] and the slaves adopted them and adapted them to make them more "African" in nature. They interpreted preparation for baptism in a way that was more closely in line with African religious rituals. The baptism of converts in the early Easter dawn according to Roman Catholic tradition allowed the slaves to celebrate the resurrection of Jesus Christ at the same time that they saluted the African god of the morning. Baptism by immersion was done in open water, which enabled the slaves to pay homage to their saint/god of the water. The post-baptismal dance, outlawed by church leaders, was subsumed by African spirit possession. Gradually however, African worship practices began to lose their definitive shape as they were incorporated into the rituals of Roman Catholicism.

As noted earlier, slaves were forbidden to participate in any form of ritual or worship that could be considered African or that was not authorized by the established church. They were required to silence the drums that had been intrinsic to their religious practices and mention of any but the Christian deity and saints was forbidden. In response, groups met in secret places at night to perform their rituals and carry out their worship. The rituals of their ancestors were passed down orally and although most could not read, with the memorization of Biblical texts and prayers taught by the monks during their indoctrination or absorbed during enforced worship times, they created a new set of rituals to meet their religious needs.

As the British took control of the colonies, "Anglican clergy ministered mainly to the plantocracy and were outrightly opposed to working among African slaves."[9] This time it meant that the slaves, and eventually the freed Blacks would have to form their own churches, providing the opportunity to create new Africana rituals. Christian Initiation was one of the most important rituals adapted from Roman Catholicism and Africanized by the slaves. Baptism was held very highly as the rite of initiation into the Christian faith. The church leaders felt very strongly that "baptism is the first requirement of those who are called or chosen to join the faith. Such initiation is an introduction to walk in God's way and to follow His will, to divorce oneself from the carnal, and to follow elements of spiritualism, putting down Adam, the first in flesh, and being raised in the newness of Christ . . ."[10] In the same way that Early Church initiates were prepared during the forty days of Lent for baptism at sunrise on Easter Sunday, these initiates underwent a similar period of preparation, but initiates were taught during their preparatory period to seek and welcome spirit possession. The spirits of erstwhile African gods became the Holy Spirit of the Christian Church. Spirit possession was evidenced as the person began to shake and shout in the same manner that was venerated by the Africans in their native religions. This manifestation of spirit possession is what earned the group the name *Shouters.*

The baptism ritual of the *Shouters* contained many elements of the early church rituals of Christian Initiation such as the washing and anointing of the baptismal candidate prior to their entrance into the water, the sealing[11] of the candidate, the dressing of the candidate before baptism in dark clothes and re-dressing after baptism in pure white clothing, baptizing in running water as in a river or sea, the announcement of the candidate with the ringing of a bell, and the introduction of the baptized person to the church by a libation at the door and the four corners of the church. Where the ritual was Africanized and in essence created for an Africana context was less in its performance than in its meaning. The ritual washing of the candidate, still a rite of preparation took on an exorcistic nature as the ritual served to remove any existing demons from the person of the candidate. Where in early church ritual the baptized person had been given a candle symbolic of the light of Christ, in its Africana context the candle represented also the passage of human life as the burning wick caused the wax to melt and the candle to grow smaller. The pre-baptism preparatory fast of candidates defined in early church ritual became in addition a process of emptying the body in preparation for spirit possession. And as stated earlier, the time and place of sunrise and running water provided a setting for acknowledgement of and obeisance, if not actual worship, to the ancestral and divine spirits of their African roots.

The creation of Africana rituals was an essential element of the preservation of both individuals and the society by and for a people who had been ripped from their religious and worship foundations. These rituals helped to preserve their identity and served as a much-needed connection to their religious roots. They helped to connect an oppressed people with the freedom of their homeland. The slaves were able to assimilate the Christian teachings of the monks into their own religion, and they adapted their worship to the dictates of Christianity such that their masters were put at ease and the slaves found solace in a worship style that reminded them of home. The adaptation of their own religious mores to the things of their new world also enabled them to present a façade of cooperation and compliance with the demands of their masters.

The ruling class and the established society of Trinidad condemned the religious practices of the *Shouters*. They developed legal statutes and executed reprisals aimed at preventing the *Shouters* from worshipping openly, but like their ancestors during slavery, the *Shouters* simply moved their Africana worship underground. Baptismal sites became well-kept secrets and even information about date, place, and time of scheduled baptisms became closely guarded secrets, provided only to members of the church on a need-to-know basis. And despite the persecution of church leaders and members, the *Shouters* continued to flourish and grow in numbers.

The retributive laws were formally repealed on July 28, 1965, however this sect of Christianity is still considered a cult by many and in some cases is even considered not totally Christian. This is due in part to the fact that, like the people to whom Jesus spoke, the *Shouters* were generally poor people of low education and of little to no status in society.

Religious ritual develops when, over time, persons hold fast to the practices that speak to and for them of the presence of a Higher Being that has power over their existence and is therefore worthy of worship. As Grimes says, "ritual is as old as humanity"[12] and Africana worship rituals have been created from religious observances and celebrations that began a long time ago in another place, and have been passed on in spite of the restrictive and demeaning experiences of those that have traveled the compendium of time and space. They offer those who observe them a way that acknowledges and honors their African history as they seek to worship the one Supreme Being, God Almighty. They are tools that allow adherents to recognize the foundations of a religious heritage that is steeped in the traditions of the motherland of Africa; to engage in the worship of the living God and experience God's presence in the fullness of their identity as persons of African origin. These rituals cause those who practice them to engage an African identity as intrinsic to the substance of their worship as the worship is to the salvation of their souls.

Notes

[1] Ronald L. Grimes, *Beginnings in Ritual Studies* (Columbia, South Carolina: University of South Carolina Press, 1995), Introduction.

[2] Gennifer Benjamin Brooks, "Preaching: A Liturgical" Act in *Circuit Rider* (January/February 2006, 11–12).

[3] Dale Bisnauth, *History of Religions in the Caribbean* (Trenton, NJ: Africa World Press, 1996), 82.

[4] John W. Pulis, *Religion, Diaspora, and Cultural Identity: A Reader in the Anglophone Caribbean* (Malaysia: Gordon and Breach Publishers, 1999), 17.

[5] Bisnauth, 86.

[6] Ibid, 87.

[7] The term "Africana" is used to represent practices and elements that are founded from, rooted in, or developed on the basis of a connection to the continent of Africa. It seeks to identify the influence of Africa on the people and culture of all who claim Africa and its peoples as foundational to their identity.

[8] The Early Church refers roughly to the period that begins at the end of the first century and goes to the fifth century in the development of the Christian Church. This is the period following the Apostolic Age of the Church.

[9] Pulis, 15.

[10] Rt. Rev. Eudora Thomas, *A History of the Shouter Baptists in Trinidad & Tobago* (Ithaca, NY: Calaloux Publications), 48.
[11] Sealing refers to the practice of writing particular Christian symbols on designated areas of the body. This may be done with chalk or the wax of a cold candle.
[12] Grimes, xxiv.

The African American Church and Sacraments: But Can We Still Get Our "Circament?"[1]

William B. McClain

If you have ever listened closely to a serious southern black Methodist, you have heard the word "circament." If you are not careful, you'll hear it from the Baptists, the few African American Presbyterians and other black protestants. At least, if they are from the part of North Alabama where I came from. But I don't think it is peculiar to that particular part of the South. I also heard it in Georgia and South Carolina, and even Massachusetts. I think it's a black southern way of referring to Holy Communion, the Lord's Supper, the Eucharist.

Just recently I was in a city in the Midwest, along with some other members of my family, visiting one of my older sisters and remaining through the weekend that happened to fall on the first Sunday of the month. And I heard it again. I heard her say in very emphatic and non-negotiable terms that the schedule for the day was that we were first going to church: "It's first Sunday and we are having Communion. I've got to go to church to get my 'circament.'" Now engaged in a ministry of teaching in a theological seminary, and teaching liturgy and preaching at that, I had not remembered hearing "circament" for a very long time. But I had heard it before, and many times in my childhood and the early years of my ministry in Alabama and later Massachusetts. Perhaps I said it, too. Just hearing the word and the expression brought back many memories. Memories of my Aunt (always pronounced "Aint" in the South) Minnie and my Cousin Cathaleen and Mr. Eddie Stamps, Brother Bob Johnson (a "steward" known to all for his stirring prayers), and Miss Margaret Wofford (who always saw to it that there were beautiful white flowers in the chancel and on the altar), and Sweet Home M.E. Church in spite of the 1939 reunification and mergers (all of which they were quite aware of), they insisted on distinguishing themselves as a part of the Northern church, as opposed to the Methodist Church South or the various branches of the African American Methodist bodies), and memories of "blueing" bleach applied to white dresses to make them pure white uniforms, Argo-starched and flat ironed to absolute perfection, worn only for that special occasion. And a special occasion it was; it was **Communion Sunday** *every* first Sunday.

That Sunday was different from any other Sunday of the month. I could always tell because my Aunt Minnie, who helped to raise me, was a Communion steward and her uniform was hanging on the nail on the wall Saturday night in readiness for her to "serve" the next day. Breakfast at home was hurried on that Sunday morning with no chance to get the usual second helpings. She had a task to perform, a duty to carry out, she had to **be there** to prepare the "circament" and wait the table and assist Rev. Carson or Coleman, or whoever the Elder was, in this important monthly service.

The church was always full on the first Sunday, for the "faithful" members of Sweet Home–even if they were not there other Sundays–dared not miss the **first** Sunday, the chance "to get their circament." Miss any other Sunday of the month, if you must, but not the first Sunday. They had to be there to "get their "circament."

I am not absolutely certain where the term "circament" came from. My best guess is that it is a combination of the words "circuit" and "sacrament." In the early days of Methodism, many of the black churches (and a much larger number of white churches, too) were served by local pastors, exhorters, local deacons and lay preachers who performed a yeoman service, and kept many small churches open and alive. These lay preachers were authorized to do virtually everything a pastor could or needed to do. I don't think they have ever been given credit and recognition for the great service they rendered to the church and the cause of Christianity, especially in rural areas and small towns, North, South, and Midwest. They could conduct worship, preach, conduct class meetings, perform marriages, visit the sick, shut-ins, widows and orphans, and bury the dead, but the one thing they *could not do* was to celebrate Communion. That required an elder. And since many of the churches were on a circuit (several churches assigned to a fully ordained minister), the elder would not be present at each church every Sunday. So when the "circuit-riding" elder got to the church, he (there were no women elders in those days) would celebrate the sacrament of Communion and offer what probably came to be known as the "circament."

A few months ago I was in West Virginia conducting a preaching mission and workshop on preaching and worship. I was making the point in the workshop on how important the celebration of Communion is in the African American churches of all denominations, but especially those with Methodist ties, i.e., African Methodist Episcopal, AME Zion, Christian Methodist Episcopal, etc., when one of the white pastors attending interrupted me to say: "That's not true of our churches here in West Virginia. In one of the churches I serve you can't even serve Communion in the sanctuary, and certainly not during the regular service. We do that in the small chapel either before the service or after the service." I was shocked.

For some time I have been aware that many white churches do not place the importance on the Eucharist that the black churches do. I suspect and hope that, with many of the changes that have taken place as a result of liturgical renewal, the use of the Common Lectionary, modifications in the Communion liturgy itself, the new hymnals, and so on, that the pattern is beginning to change. But many white pastors and students have reported to me over the years in my teaching in theological seminaries that their experience is the exact opposite of mine in the black church: Communion Sunday is their Sunday of lowest attendance.

Even though my sister now belongs to one of the remaining thriving, large, sophisticated, predominantly white, downtown "cathedral-like" United Methodist churches, with paid soloists and accomplished organists (the Buxtehude fugue and Boellmann postlude were magnificent!) and other musicians, highly literate pastors who make copies of their sermons available to the worshiping congregation immediately after being "delivered," a very strong and effective outreach program to missions and the surrounding community, she still feels strongly about **getting her "circament,"** and complains that it is not celebrated nearly often enough (not every first Sunday).

Not celebrating the Holy Communion regularly, and at least on the *first* Sunday, deprives my sister of one of the privileges of punctuating her dignity.

And she is not a "bench warmer" member. She works in the church (as we would say back home), and that very Sunday her husband had left us behind much earlier, even before we could have a second cup of coffee together, because he had to be there to usher. It was the first Sunday and that is Communion Sunday!

What is the difference here and why is there such an emphasis on the celebration of the sacrament of Holy Communion in the black church and the importance of preaching on that day? Why is the attendance the highest for the month (and the offering, too)? What accounts for it being the Sunday of importance it is in the black church and not the white church? Why did my sister insist on getting her "circament"?

I suspect the first part of answering these questions is that the celebration of Communion in the white church has been the sheer absence of **celebration**. So often it has been viewed as a service of utter solemnity, quietness, and ritualism with a minimum of congregational participation. And far too often, it has been viewed by the clergy as a long, arid ritual "something for them to get through." Consequently, the service has been conducted in that fashion with the attitude of the erstwhile "celebrant" coming through.

When the Communion is approached this way there can be no celebration. Instead of a high, holy, expectant and exciting festive service, it becomes liturgical "ho-hum," ritualistic tedium, and boredom for both the leader and the congregation.

A second part of it is probably theological. The Sunday service of Communion in celebration of the resurrection of Christ and the victory of Christ over sin and death is seen as a **Friday funeral service for a dead Jesus.** Therefore, quietness and solemnity is required, as is seen appropriate for funerals. But the black church approaches this service differently. It is not viewed as a funeral. It is not even usually seen merely as a memorial meal. Rather, it is a time of joyful celebration of the victorious risen Christ over sin and death and all of the powers of evil and hell! It is not still Friday with all of its gloom, suffering and death. It is Sunday, the day of his rising and our rising, his victory and ours because of his triumph. We've come through Friday–and we must go through Friday–with all of its pain and suffering, its hellish ways and ours, the scourging and death, but God sends Sunday with the uncontradictory signal of victory. Sunday has come–now a special Sunday–to celebrate the victory of God & Company over the sinister powers of Pilate and the Good Friday crowd. God claimed the victory and shared it with us all, Hallelujah! It is time to sing joyfully–even lustily–to praise God in acts of triumph of the risen Christ.

I am not suggesting that the preacher has to leap off the pinnacle of the temple; nor am I inferring that there has to be a bag of gimmicks or tricks or imitative magic. Nor is "planned spontaneity" called for–not then, or ever; but expectancy, participation, hope, and celebration are in order–even required! What I am suggesting is that there is reason for celebration and joy: that in "getting our circament," we are remembering the great gift and receiving it all over again, and we show gratitude in a "much-obliged" way–acknowledging the gift of grace with gratitude while obligating and committing and re-committing ourselves to his way of living, a life of obedience and service, a life of discipleship, engaging in acts of compassion, charity and justice.

In black United Methodist churches, the historic confession of the Christian faith, the Apostles' Creed is recited (I say recited because it has been memorized by all of the faithful) and has a prominent place in the ritual. I was always amazed as a child that my Aunt Minnie, and so many like her who could neither read nor write, knew every single word of that creed and stood and majestically and with forthrightness, if not with a bit of religious pride, declared their faith. I seldom celebrate or participate in the "circament" nowadays without being reminded of her and her role at the Communion table. I feel joined to her and those who came faithfully to Sweet Home, as I repeat those ancient words that I learned from her lips: **"I believe in . . . the communion of the saints."**

Preaching is always a very real and central part of the celebration of the Eucharist. In the black church it is, in fact–and by good intention–**Word and Sacrament.** It is preaching, not meditations or "sermonettes for Christianettes" or merely even short homilies, but the preaching of the Word with preparation and passion. Any pastor of these African American churches needs to know that his or her best sermon of the month ought to be prepared and delivered on Communion Sunday! What better time is there to declare that God was in Christ reconciling the world unto God's self? What better time is there to help us to see and confess the depth of our sin, the variety and abundance of our dissembling with one another, and to proclaim the mysteriously extravagant riches of God's grace and the wonder of God's forgiving love? When is there a better time to preach as a guilty one telling other guilty ones of the judgment of God upon us, but also of a love that is wider than the judgment and a mercy that is kinder than justice? What better liturgical moment is there to remind the people and ourselves that God wants back what belongs to God? For in a real sense, the celebration of Communion is a "party for prodigals" who have fallen on their knees, some in the swine pens way away from home, some who have wallowed in smugness and self-righteousness at home, but all can come back to take a seat at the place that has been saved for them at the banquet table.

At the Communion service is an open and ready opportunity no, the responsibility!–for the preacher to preach judgment and grace, law and love, sin and forgiveness, a satisfying and slaking word to those who hunger and thirst. Or as the great Daniel Thambryrajah (always understandably called "D.T.") Niles defined evangelism, which was for him the same as preaching: "one beggar telling another beggar where you found bread." And in the black church the people come on Communion Sunday asking for and expecting that bread. It happens so very often and in so many diverse places, with utter joy and fulfillment, that the Bread of Life and the Bread of Heaven are offered together and the people leave Communion filled.

In the African American churches **we always sing** while the circament is offered. And, in most of those churches, including small and rural ones, the responses are sung. Even the hymns of passion and suffering become songs of praise and celebration. You've never heard such hymns as "Jesus Keep Me Near the Cross," "Come Ye Disconsolate," and "There Is A Fountain Filled With Blood" (one reason it had to remain in the new United Methodist Hymnal), sung so joyfully. The old African American spiritual, so very often sung at this holy celebration, is appropriate: "Let Us Break Bread Together on Our Knees," for it climaxes with the joyful admonition: "Let us praise God together on our knees!" For we are aware of why the suffering takes place and what is on the other side of the pain and the crucifixion. It is not crucifying Friday now; it's Communion Sunday, the day of resurrection!

It is this recognition that in the reality of the shedding of the blood of Jesus, and the brokenness of his body has become our own liberation from sin and death, and the slavery the world can impose on those who put their true trust in its trinkets and treasures.

Or, as we used to always sing after Communion in Union Church in Boston where I once pastored:

> My sin, oh, the bliss of this glorious thought!
> My sin, not in part but the whole
> Is nailed to the cross and I bear it no more,
> Praise the Lord, praise the Lord, O my soul!
>
> It is well with my soul.
> It is well, it is well with my soul.[2]

At the celebration of Communion our hunger and thirst were satisfied. Our lives were restored and we left energized, enabled, empowered, and compelled to witness to all, that He is a heart-fixer, a mind-regulator and an attitude-adjuster who requires all who call his name and accept his grace to show forth his love, and work for peace and justice in the land.

No wonder my sister insisted on us going to church to "get our 'circament.'" We left renewed and reunited. And we all said: "I'm sure glad she made us go today!" I hope that experience is repeated willingly by millions upon millions–and very often.

Notes

[1] This article previously appeared in the March-April 1997 issue of *Worship Arts* as "The Importance of Holy Communion: The African American Church and the 'Circament,'" and is reprinted with the author's permission.
[2] Horatio G. Spafford, "It Is Well with My Soul" (Stanza 3), 1873.

Death as Worship: Celebrating Dying As Part of Life[1]

CHERYL KIRK-DUGGAN

Death: Just a Breath Away

Life and death
Point, counterpoint
Face-off each moment:
between inhale and exhale.

Between each breath we take,
People live, People die
Life comes
Death takes no holiday,
But visits:
noisily, quietly, repulsively, peacefully, enigmatically–
Where did all that hot air go?

Butterflies fly
Death comes.
Praise, Adore, Embody God: Live life.
Die, dead, expire.
Death of me, of you
When we let oppression
Snuff out our life force: our ideas, actions,
Our being:
Gloria in excelsis Deo!

Our essence
Exits stage left.
We allow
Things and people
To break our sweet communion
with God, three in One–Unadulterated theft.

I held her hand as she died. Fifty years before God had breathed life into her and she became a living being. I sang a few songs, read Scripture, and prayed. I told her to breathe down. She inhaled the Holy Spirit, exhaled all pain and suffering, and died. I saw breath and life leave and death enter in. The nurse confirmed that she was dead. We called family members from the hall into the room to say good-bye. A nurse phoned members of our prayer band. Together, as a true body of Christ, we experienced death as worship. The Refining Fire of God had molded a cooling board for our friend.

Death: A Turnstile to the Unknown

Death, a turnstile to the unknown, is a rich, powerful, and painful cultural and theological experience that Refines the Fires of ultimate joyous encounter. Death is the way station of life that follows incarnated life,[1] when living and breathing consciousness has ceased. For the living dead, those who still breathe, physical death may or may not be the same type of experience; they are alive, but the depths of their woundedness, oppression, and resulting self-hatred deadens their spirits and vitality, their humanness. Death, the ultimate measure of life, is a door to active eternal life. Christians believe that God created them *imago dei*. That belief permits us to choose to experience Christian life and Christian death as liturgical celebrations, as worship.

Liturgy is thinking about and embodying God, creation, salvation, and other doctrines or beliefs into the context of worship and prayer. The worship experience is the adoration, praise, and thanksgiving to God for God's grace and glory by the corporate, gathered community. Using the liturgical experience as a metaphor illumines the relationship between death, life, and God as worship.

This chapter, in order to explore death as worship, uses liturgical expressions and seasons with their liturgical colors and the experience of certain moments during the worship service as moments of Refining divine Fires of praise and inspiration. That is, we explore the celebration of transition to eternal life by the African American Christian community from a Womanist perspective. In traditional African Culture and in the Christian experience, death is transition and may be transforming. The mood of this chapter reflects a liturgical hermeneutic that integrates the writing and reading of this work into an act of praise. This hermeneutical or interpretative methodological dialogue of praise becomes a litany. The antiphonal moments engage my text with excerpts of Womanist poetry as response.

> . . . and only those who stay dead
> Shall remember death.
>
> Audre Lorde[2]

Death: A Transition of Time-Ordered Life

Death is a transition or translation of time-ordered life, but is not the absence of life. When we come together as children of God and stand next to the body of our beloved friend, we are multiracial, ecumenical, female and male, and diverse socio-economic classes. We gather in an act of praise, a profound liturgical moment of shifting realities. Amid joy and sorrow, we lay hands on her once again. Many times before, we had sung, read Scripture, and prayed together, had brought her food and drink, and took her to treatment centers. We had lived and Refined the Fires of compassion, generosity, and love. She had fought her disease and daily claimed her healing triumph in the Lord. Her courage allowed her to do the unbelievable. She led a normal life in the agony of terminal suffering. She gave her last recital, despite a medical death sentence, and her regal demeanor endured midst suffering and cloaked her in death. We celebrate her life and death as the process of living and ultimate healing. We cry and rejoice. She died. We are all in transition. Death is an ultimate transition, a mysterious journey refining the fires of immortality and difference.

Is Death the Enemy or a Pilgrimage of Joy?

This mysterious rite of passage becomes an experience of terror when death is the enemy. Death is a pilgrimage of joy when one knows that both life and death are gifts. Death brings humanity more fully into God's presence; thus, death is liberating. Death is inevitable, and it affects every area of our lives. Yet, we distance ourselves from death by worshipping youthfulness, immortality, and materialism. Examples of such distancing include the increased number of deaths at hospitals and sterile care facilities in the presence of strangers, instead of at home, in the presence of family and friends. This is not to say that we cannot be surrounded by love, relatives, and friends when the monumental nature of illness and dying demands that one is hospitalized. Once life is no longer present, an entire industry strives to make the dead corpse lifelike with the appearance of sleep or rest, a denial that death has visited the human.

The implicit denial of death and human finitude, the social abhorrence of death as a topic of conversation, is the dis-ease of ageism: the marginalization, discrimination, and exclusive behavior by persons and institutions. By facing the reality of death, we confront and combat human frailty, loneliness, feelings of dispensability, and actual incapacitation of aging with love. We combat the feelings of fear and meaninglessness by celebrating the God-presence in every aging person. We Refine the Fires of wellness and contentment when we fully grasp that every person at each stage of her or his life is sacred, holy. The responsibility of all communities is to celebrate this holy life and help us remember who each person is. Then we can embrace the dying person as necessary, wanted, and vital even when facing the awesomeness and often agony of the dying process. Death itself is a quiet release. To refuse to engage and minister to aging and dying persons is to violate one's own personhood and to forget that life itself is a gift. Life continuously evolves and embraces the fact that all who are born die.

A few years ago, I gave last rites to a beautiful 106-year-old spirit: what a privilege and a gift to stand at the bedside of one who had lived a thousand, thousand days. Those moments felt as if time was suspended. Nothing else mattered, but sharing all the love, gentleness, and nobility that I could with an ancient, sweet soul. In that moment she and I were between the now and not yet, an eschatological moment of grace.

Life and Death Are Eschatological

Awareness about the essence of who we are and whose we are in life and death is eschatological. An eschatological life is one in which the experiences, visions, and ethics as praxis define how one deals with aging, the immediacy of death, and finitude. Seeing how we live in the now illumines and reflects what we expect to happen in our last days and in eternity. The goals of our life signal our sense of realized eschatology: that which we experience now shapes and manifests now and in the future. An eschatological sense of death has far reaching implications for all to expand beyond the experience of last things to daily goals, visions, and ethical imperatives. An eschatological view places life next to, around, and beside death. The collision of that confrontation can be either overwhelming or liberating when made pertinent to God's presence in individual and corporate life. Death is real, and it laughs in the face of mortality. Being mortal and spirit, we are "ecclesiastic" people–people fueled by the Holy Spirit and shaped by natural cycles and experiences of time. The life encounter expressed liturgically Refines the Fires of death as a moment for empowerment, tranquility, and reflection.

Liturgical Seasons: Life Processes

A Womanist experience of the liturgical seasons embraces African American folk culture, the socio-political and religious ramifications of black life, within the historical context of life and death. These encounters embrace the experiences and issues of black women in life and literature as rituals of empowerment and liberation. Such rituals embrace celebration and social protest. Womanist thought gives voice to those silenced by the oppression of race/sex/class differences and gives voice with the tools and ideologies informed by history, economics, theology, and biblical witness. Womanist theory requires a universalist temperament. That universalism Refines the Fires of human self-expression as one who can love all people, as one who is outrageous and creatively embraces life that hinges on the survival and wholeness of all people.[3]

> . . . in memory of the bitter hours when we discovered we were
> black and poor
> and small and different and nobody cared and nobody won-
> dered . . .
>
> Margaret Walker[4]

Such a view of death requires that people remember the liberation traditions of black folk culture and community. We remember the personhood of women and men in our communities as we acknowledge all age groups and persons. We engage their voices and celebrate their thoughts and faith experiences that have enabled humanity to survive as the oppressions of racism, sexism, classism, and ageism have made most of us face off death moments on a daily basis. A Womanist study of death as worship is a rhythmic dance of

Advent, Christmastide, Epiphany, Lent, Eastertide, and Pentecost. These seasons, moments of complex Refining Fires, mirror the Christian life process.

The Advent Season

Advent begins with the fourth Sunday before Christmas. During this season, Christians rehearse the first coming of Christ, of the Incarnation, of God become human and await the coming of Christ in final judgment. Many observe this joyous, redemptive season as a time for prayer and fasting. We experience the Advent of persons and events: of Christ, of new babies, of transitional periods, of growth. Some get caught in the consumerism that can drown out the honest, simple beauty of this season. During antebellum slavery, the birth of each new babe was followed by the question, "Is this child the one, the one who will lead us out of bondage?" In contemporary African American communities, the Advents of new life experiences and death are constant. Death can and has visited us at the moment of birth, when the child leaves the womb and enters the world. Womanists anticipate and embrace this life and death dialectic. Womanists envision new life as a healthy community that welcomes the birth of equality and the death of racism/sexism/classism.

The royal color purple symbolizes both the Womanist experience and the solemn anticipation of Advent. Purple depicts majesty and heralds Christ's coming. This anticipatory sense invites us to note the majesty in all humanity, in life, and in death. For God loves "a mess of stuff [we] don't . . . . [God wants us] to share a good thing . . . . It pisses god [*sic*] off if you walk by the color purple in a field somewhere and don't notice it."[5] What kinds of rituals can we create to help people experience the color purple as they cross over life's joyful or painful hurdles and over the chilly and liberating Jordan? Suffering persons with deep spirituality and a strong God presence anticipate their imminent encounter with death. What about the living dead, alive to addictions and hopelessness, but dead to life itself? How do we help them Refine the Fires illumined by the color purple and thus anticipate transformation and renewal?

> let her be born
> & handled warmly.
>
> Ntozake Shange[6]

Christmastide

Christmastide, the liturgical feast that celebrates the birth of Jesus, is the day that honors the gift of life, renewal, and God's incarnated love and mercy.

This embodied light and hope of the world glows brightly. God's radiance eclipses the glare caused by the commercialization of Christmas. The true sense of the Christ-mass is the celebration of God's love in concert with human good will and the praxis of building relationships and family. Birth is the gateway to family.

Families–biological, extended, and/or created–are the context of lives conjoined: patterns of behavior, symphonies of voices, complexities and myths that juxtapose the real with the ideal. Physical, spiritual, emotional, and socio-psychological births or rebirths offer opportunities for transforming anger, violence, denial, domination, subordination, and patriarchal kinships into intimacy, egalitarianism, *agape*, mutuality, and respect. Birth evokes memory, and memory recreates the family–ancestors, contemporaries, the yet unborn. A concept of family that births an empowering attitude about the recontextualization of the African American family within an oppressive society can move us toward wholeness. In our society, children are not born with hate, but institutions and sick families quickly imbue infants with notions of otherness and inferiority. A Womanist view of the family sees and celebrates difference and similarity. Fear, ignorance, and the need to control thrive on subjugation of "those people," of others, and make difference pathological. That pathology issues a death warrant to mutuality and love of neighbor.

Christmas offers an alternative prognosis. Christmas does not deny reality but Refines the Fires of possibility for attitude adjustments and transformation. The color white, the color for Christmas and Epiphany, the color of innocence and virginity, symbolizes the potential for magnificence that is in Christmas and Epiphany. Christmas and Epiphany refract the light of God that shines in every human being. Christmas awakens the opportunity; Epiphany makes the pronouncement.

Epiphany

Epiphany is the church festival that observes the coming of the Magi as the first recognition of Christ by the Gentiles, or in the Eastern Church, the baptism of Christ. This manifestation or pronounced reality echoes the power of the spoken word. The Magi, like God, spoke and that which was stated–the Logos–came into being. The spoken word brings forth and begets reality. The power of speech creates but can also destroy. Words become living entities, bringing life, death, or both. Words are bits of language. Language makes up conversation. Conversations for action are the crux of reality and can change the world.[7] The words of Epiphany live via signifying. In the black vernacular, signifying is a rhetorical strategy or language game of double voicing. Double voicing embraces repetition, revision, and intertextuality, to express simultaneously meanings of an original utterance and multiple other meanings. This process draws upon the sounds of words as opposed to their meanings.

The signification of Epiphany is the adult naming and encoding ritual, the meta-discourse, that affords a black rhetorical process of difference and independence. Signifying, a figure of speech is a trope that details the life and death processes integral to being and existence. Health care practitioners signify the actuality, time, place, and date of birth and death. Birth and death certificates codify these significations. Epiphany invites us to signify or pronounce life and accept death in faith, Refining the Fires of existence as gift. Christian faith signifies death as confession, not explanation. Such faith teaches that physical death limits humanity but is not inherently evil. Physical death lets us know life and God in a different way. Spiritual death and human anxiety about physical death separate us from God. The confession of Epiphany is the mystery of life and death embodied within the incarnated Christ Jesus.

> Evil is no black thing: black . . .
> of death, but not its essence:
>
> Sarah Webster Fabio[8]

Lent

The Lenten season is forty days long, forty days[9] that echo Jesus' time in the wilderness during his fasting and meditation, from Ash Wednesday to Easter Sunday. Lent evolved from a time of preparation for the Easter baptism, when the catechumens received instruction, fasted, and prayed, to a time when many Christians today observe penitence, fasting, thanksgiving, and reflections concerning God's promises. This reflection time allows one to contemplate personal and corporate sin, or living death, and move toward penitence and forgiveness. The juxtaposition of life and death at the cross on Good Friday creates a paradox, a dialectic of the now and the not yet. Each year, many give up or deny themselves a particular habit, pleasure, or experience as a means of distancing themselves from worldly pleasures, Refining the Fires of discipline and asceticism. This period of active fasting and waiting is an effort to prepare their hearts, to abstain from self, and to move toward a higher spiritual plane. Lent is a time to die to the secular and draw toward the sacrality of life. From a Womanist perspective, Lent is a time to test personal wholeness: a time to acknowledge betrayals, losses, alienation; a time to pray for the willingness to experience and offer God's forgiving grace and sustaining love.

During these reflective moments, an individual contemplates the previous instances of sin or living death as she or he repents, seeks divine forgiveness, and moves toward transformation. Lent is a corporate and an individual wilderness experience. The forty days embrace an Exodus motif in which one moves from Egypt to the Promised Land. The eminence of Good Friday sets a tone for one who wants new life. The cross stands ominously within a dialectic of despair and hope.

Many recognize the cross but question the whole nature of atonement, of being renewed to God. Some concede that the life-giving blood sacrifice, required for atonement, resulted in Jesus' death. Many ask how could a loving God require the death of any child, particularly the Child of the Divine? Some thus argue for focusing more on the revolutionary, life-giving ministry of Jesus as opposed to focusing on his death and then allowing oneself to be abused because one is allegedly carrying a cross. Some recognize the cross not as a sanctioning of violence and suffering but as testimony to such evil and as transformation.

Wherever one stands on atonement, every moment that we live brings us closer to our physical death. Every moment that we live is also an opportunity for our spiritual life. Amid the purple that symbolizes Lent, we all wait at the foot of all crosses, self-imposed and otherwise, and look and listen to receive Easter Sunday's good news. Lent opens us to a process of releasing Womanist melodies that embrace God's spirit as we struggle with trying to live harmoniously and to engage our critical voices within fragile personhood and a social order rife with double consciousness. Our purple lens enables us to set aside the mundane and awakens a hopeful imagination toward experiencing the glory of God amid the newness and the Resurrection, toward healing.

> How can I mourn these children . . .
> Young do not dream of dying . . .
>
> Audre Lorde[10]

Eastertide

Resurrection is the activity of Eastertide. Eastertide begins with Easter Sunday and concludes on Pentecost. East celebrates life restored to a world previously devastated by sin. Easter implies the opportunity for recovery and Refines the Fires of life as gift, in which one celebrates this gift of choosing to live. Easter shares the reality that God is in charge and that life is God's gift to us. A true experience of Easter makes one uncomfortable and unwilling to remain in unhealthy relationships with self, God, and others, and a true experience of

Easter reminds us that we cannot deny what we need to do to take care of ourselves. Easter is the manifestation of *agape*, love in action. The redemptive spirit of Easter pushes us toward gratitude and beyond the need to punish the other. Punitive otherness is a result of separation and ignorance. Easter strikes the death knell to the evils of separation, ignorance, idolatry, and sin. *"mortis formidine, vitae percepit humanos odioum lucisque videndae"* (for fear of death human beings are seized by hatred of life and of seeing the light).[11] Having any person, place, or thing as ultimate concern other than God is idolatry. To have victimhood or egoism as the generating life source also intones idolatry. Easter confronts this idolatry, Refining the Fires of paradox–the tension between sin and grace.

This confrontation between sing and grace reorders individual and communal life experiences toward championing the sacrality of life. Life, as a sacramental confession, relies on rituals of penance and mercy. Easter worship involves rituals and symbols that focus on the ecclesial and Christological reality of human life. Placing the church, the body of Christ, and the eternal Jesus Christ at the center of Christian life is an invitation for a life of service. A life that embraces altruistic behavior and Christian service is a most promising ethos and praxis for Christian leadership and discipleship. This resurrection lifestyle reconstructs reality and leads to socio-cultural, religious, and political solidarity. The color white,[12] a symbol of innocence, symbolizes the risen Christ's radiance, the living light and hope for all those who thirst for living water along with the solidarity of the Easter triumph over sin, suffering, and death.

The liberating force of Christian Womanist theology recognizes that Easter grants us the permission and in fact demands that we preach, teach, and practice a theology that posits a holistic, integrated reality of African American womanhood, the wholeness of black women and ultimately of all women and men. Easter says "No!" to all forms of subjugation and destruction, including socio-economic oppression. Easter yes "Yes!" to the concerns of the "least of these" for "all of us!" The Easter commemoration Refines the Fires of resurrection love, making us fishers (evangelists) of people. Our theology and ethics demand that now is the time to "fish or cut bait" through the empowerment of the Holy Spirit.

> I took a breath . . .
> I was sister . . .
>
> Johari Amini (Jewel C. Larimore)[13]

Pentecost

Christians move from Eastertide to celebrate the outpouring of the Holy Spirit during Pentecost, a word derived from the Greek term *pentekostos* applied to the fiftieth day after Passover, the Christian anniversary of the coming of the Holy Spirit. The Pentecost feast represents the manifestation of divine power and the beginning of the church. Passover marked the beginning of the harvest season; Pentecost, the Feast of Weeks, marked the end of the harvest season, the end of the Easter Refining Fire. At Pentecost, the Holy Spirit descended upon a group of 120 praying disciples, for Jesus told them to remain in Jerusalem until they received divine power. As the Holy Spirit descended upon them, via the sound of great winds and tongues of fire, the disciples began to speak in many other languages, so all could listen in their own languages, and these 120 disciples began to preach boldly in the name of Jesus the Christ.

The Holy Spirit Refines the Fires of empowerment, advocacy, and revitalization. Red, the liturgical symbol for Pentecost, depicts these flames and the outpouring of the power on the disciples. The color red represents the gifts of the outpouring: empowerment, expansion, and rebirth. Pentecost, from eleven to sixteen Sundays beginning with Pentecost Sunday, symbolizes the new life that combats living death. The red flames of expansion inspire humanity to desire healing and move actively toward transformation. The rebirth experience is the manifestation of people receiving the anointing. An anointed life is a life of awareness–the awareness of powers and principalities. An anointed life Refines the Fires of opportunity to know peace while living midst the dialectic of flesh and spirit. (Kingdom-tide is often symbolized by the color green, which depicts the prosperity of harvest time, and is often subsumed under the Pentecost season, which continues until Advent.) Pentecost is a time of embracing newness that does not fear death. Pentecost anticipates possibility and welcomes the intimacy of a spirit-filled life in Christ. A Womanist vision of Pentecost Refines the Fires of healing old wounds and celebrates life as an unfolding journey and death as a consequence of life.

> the meaning . . .
> [is] unfolding.
>
> Alice Walker[14]

Liturgical Moments: Death as Process

The liturgical seasons reflect a life and death experience of mystery, miracle, and empowerment. We can describe what happens at birth and death, but we do not really know what happens. We see the wonderment of the miraculous realities and possibilities in a spiritual life in relationship. Relationships are paramount to life. Without relationships one can only know death. We also see the result of Refining the Fires of authority: changed attitudes, changed visions, and changed lives. The embodiment of mystery, miracle and empowerment within human life undergirds liturgical moments of the worship service. In viewing selected liturgical moments common to many Protestant, Orthodox, and Roman Catholic worship services, we see that these liturgical moments parallel the human life/death experience as a procession toward the praise and adoration of God, which ends with a sending forth to live

The Processional

The introit or processional of the worship service is the moving toward God through Christ Jesus and the movement in life toward death. The candle lighting represents the illumination that opens us to see God and opens us to let the light of God shine through us. This illumination gives us the courage to face the injustices of life and the reality of death. Death moves us toward eternal life. The greeting and call to worship invite the congregation to focus on the adoration of God. The adoration and praise of God always encourages us to be at one with God as a community of faith. Such praise assures us that we are never alone. Even in death, God never forsakes us. The hymn of praise, along with other musical selections, liturgical drama, and dance, follows the dictates of the Psalmist, who invites us to praise God with every breath and every fiber and act of our being: Refining the Fires of holy embodiment.

All such creative liturgical expressions reflect the beauty of creation and provide the opportunity for fulfillment not afforded us with the onset of physical death or the separation indicative of spiritual demise. Prayers, responsive readings, affirmation of faith, and covenant statements or creeds are reactions and supplications to God. These reactions denote what we believe, what we desire, and how we are called to live. The thanksgiving and pleas common to prayer and response are the inspiring encounters that help us face daily life and death experiences. The affirming nature of worship is concretized in the giving of gifts.

Tithes, Offerings, Sermon, and Benediction

Tithes and offerings are one way we concretely give back to God and to the community of believers. Tithing of time and other gifts is critical to a full experience of life, a full experience that negates any need to deny our own morality, aging, and death.

Scripture readings feed us spiritually and provide the context for the sermon. The sermon or homily flushes out the theological and ethical implications for Christian life and discipleship. The Eucharist, also known as the Lord's Supper or Holy Communion, offers us atonement, forgiveness, freedom, and intimate relationship with God, Refining the Fires of renewal, rebirth, and reclamation of *imago dei.* The life that we life reflects our sacramental hermeneutic and preaches a sermon more striking than the words we speak. Our living sermon also says a great deal about our perspective on death.

> Death be not proud, though some have called thee . . .
> And death shall be no more; Death, thou shalt die.
>
> John Donne[15]

Life and death are two experiences on the continuum of living. Neither life nor death is necessarily fair, convenient, or predictable. There are no fixed ways to live, although ethical and moral imperatives do exist. The realities of life offer many options for our use of time, meaning, and memory. But death confronts those realities and causes problems ranging from the familial to the financial. There are no set patterns for how those left to mourn will deal with death.

Even the stages posited by Elisabeth Kübler-Ross[16] (denial and isolation, anger, bargaining, depression, acceptance), which Kübler-Ross recanted when faced with her own impending demise, are not everyone's experience of death and dying. Scholars hold opposing views as to how we should cope with death, the pattern of grief, and the place of friends, the support of fellow sufferers. Much needs to be said about ways to deal with the funeral in a manner that allows the church to proclaim a significant resurrection doctrine. We need more analysis and reflection as well as preparation of the faith community family, so that the funeral event can become a time of affirmation that invites humanity to stand before the ultimate of existence and face it with fortitude and faith, not anxiety and fear.

Womanist Liturgics: Hurting, Pain, and Grief

Womanist liturgics invite us to embrace and legitimize all hurting and pain, especially the grief process as ministry to the body of Christ. Womanist liturgics also celebrate and teach us the values of balance. Thus, just as we cannot preach the entire Bible in one sermon, we cannot fully explore all the ramifications of life and death here. We can conclude that the mysterious, miraculous, powerful experiences of life and death not only mirror each other, but also are often separated only by the giving and ceasing of breath. Womanist liturgics invite each of us to Refine the Fires of celebration and praise as we breathe, dance, adore, and pray. In so doing, we build friendships and nurture each other's souls, to live and die in the faith and love of a God who never sleeps and a God who breathes life into us.

The spirit within
Looses touch with reality,
Oh what Pain
for the Creator who never sleeps!

Yes, Jesus wept and still weeps.
The tears flow, knowing the grief
when *Imago Dei*,
Separates from the Almighty Beloved,
And from the Almighty in humanity:
The self, the neighbor,
The addict, the thief, the liar,
all who mirror you and me.
Forget bout MTV!
Are the children home?

Seasons of purple,
Red, green, white
Be present, doing praise
All are sacred in God's sight.
We are invited, without fright
To see God is here.
And what of our children?

Are they part
Of a heart too filled with
The gods of Death?
They, so close to the divine,
Still trust,
Until we deaden their souls.

But Jesus also laughs.
We laugh, and we live, and we sneeze, even as we die:
"Say Amen, Somebody!"

Notes

[1] The first and last poems are by the author. In this reprint of this chapter in *Refiner's Fire: A Religious Engagement with Violence*, Augsburg/Fortress Press, 2000, the poetry by other poets has been shortened to two lines only.
[2] Audrey Lorde, "Memorial I" in *Chosen Poems Old and New* (New York: W.W. Norton & Company, 1982) 3.
[3] Alice Walker, *In Search of Our Mothers' Gardens: Womanist Prose* (New York: Harcourt Brace Jovanovich, 1983), xi.
[4] Margaret Walker, "For My People," in Stephen Henderson, ed., *Understanding the New Black Poetry: Black Speech and Black Music as Poetic References* (New York: William Morrow, 1975) 163-65.
[5] Alice Walker, *The Color Purple* (New York: Pocket Books, 1982) 203.
[6] Ntozake Shange, *For colored girls who have considered suicide/when the rainbow is enuf: a choreopoem* (New York: Macmillan, 1977) 2.
[7] Rayona Sharpnack, "Women Leading Change," workshop at the Institute for Women's Leadership, Santa Clara, California, January, 2000.
[8] Sarah Webster Fabio,. "Evil is No Black Thing" in Stephen Henderson, ed., *Understanding the New Black Poetry*, 1973, 241-42.
[9] It also echoes the forty years that the Israelites wandered in the wilderness before entering the promised land.
[10] Audre Lorde, "Holographs," in *Our Dead Behind Us: Poems* (New York: W.W. Norton, 1994) 59-60.
[11] Lucretius Carus, *De Rerum Naturm*, III, 79 in *Anchor Book of Latin Quotations*, compiled by Norbert Guterman (New York: Anchor Books, 1990,1996) 92.
[12] White is also the color of mourning in Eastern cultures.
[13] Johari Amini, "Identity" in Henderson, 352-54.
[14] Alice Walker, "Rest in Peace" in *Horses Made a Landscape Look More Beautiful. Selected Writings, 1973-1987* (New York: Harcourt Brace Jovanovich, 1988) 88-89.
[15] See *The Oxford Dictionary of Quotations* (2d ed; London: Oxford University Press, 1955) 185; *Merriam-Webster's Encyclopedia of Literature* (Springfield, Mass.: Merriam Webster, 1995) 338.
[16] See Elisabeth Kubler-Ross, *On Death and Dying* (New York: Macmillan, 1969) and *On Life After Death* (New York: Celestial Arts, 1991); Elisabeth Kubler-Ross and Mal Warshaw, *To Live until We Say Good-bye* (Englewood Cliffs, NJ: Prentice Hall, 1982).

The African American Funeral Sermon: Divine Re-Framing of Human Tragedy[1]

FRANK A. THOMAS

One of the most memorable moments of impact in my young life was an encounter with an African American funeral sermon. I was college-aged. One of my close friends was shot and killed in a botched shoe store robbery attempt. It was shocking and devastating for the young people in our neighborhood. My friend was well loved, and the outpouring of grief was tremendous and deep. There is something about the grief of young people that is particularly painful. Maybe it is the false sense of invincibility that often parades in the guise of youth. At any rate, I remember the huge group of young people trying to come to terms with their grief. We went to the funeral and sat together five rows deep.

The preacher did something for us. We did not know what he did, but when he got through preaching we felt better. I am sure it was not the preaching singularly, but if it was any one thing, it would have been the preaching. I do not remember what he preached. I do not remember what text or what scripture he used. It has been years now. But I do remember that we all felt better. I understand now that what occurred was a divine re-framing of human tragedy.

Death and tragedy are inevitable experiences for every human being. In the midst of death and tragedy, we experience the natural emotions of grief, confusion, anger, and the inexpressible pain of separation. Re-framing is the process where one is enabled to look at tragic and painful events and emotions, and through the illumination of scripture and the presence of the Holy Spirit, see a truer spiritual reality. African American preachers help people look at the tragic through divine eyes of healing and mercy. While total re-framing is an arduous process that often takes years, it can begin with the funeral service and the African American funeral sermon. The African American preacher re-frames death, sickness, disease, and illness by assisting mourners to view tragedy from the divine perspective.

Since that time I have heard much African American funeral preaching. I have done an extensive amount of it myself. Regardless of the age, class, race, or sex of the deceased or the family, the preaching assignment has always been the same: to help people re-frame earthly tragedy by looking at events through heaven's eyes. In my book, *They Like to Never Quit Praisin' God: The Role of Celebration in Preaching*,[2] I discuss looking at events through heaven's eyes as the nature and purpose of the African American sermon. Looking at events through heaven's eyes is called the *assurance of grace*. The nature and purpose of the African American sermon is *to help people experience the assurance of grace that is the gospel of Jesus Christ*. We offer people an *assurance of grace* that enables them to re-frame tragic events and look at them through heaven's eyes.

One of the fundamental ways the African American preacher helps people experience the assurance of grace is through the last stage of the sermon labeled as celebration. In my book, I say a great deal about celebration, but the following is the definitive statement:

> Celebration is the culmination of the sermonic design, where a moment is created in which the remembrance of a redemptive past and/or the conviction of a liberated future transforms the events immediately experienced.[3]

The preacher helps the listeners to experience the remembrance of redemptive past and/or the conviction of a liberated future, and that experience re-frames the tragedy that is being immediately experienced. African American preachers, through the genius of celebration, help people see tragic events through heaven's eyes. Before the advent of psychological sciences, the African American preacher offered bereavement ministry through celebrative sermons. The genius of African American preaching has been the ability to sustain a people in the midst of the tragic by celebrating the gospel of Jesus Christ.

What is the process by which we re-frame? How does one construct a sermon to re-frame? While the scope of this article does not allow a detailed methodological discussion, the preacher must help people 1) face the stark reality of the bad news, 2) apply the gospel to the bad news, and 3) celebrate the gospel.

Step One: Face the Stark Reality of the Death, Tragedy, or Bad News

The preacher must help persons to face the stark reality of loss and separation. Many people have only partially begun to accept the reality of death. Because, especially during a funeral, the church is a safe place, if the preacher gently and skillfully prods, many people will allow themselves to feel, as much as they can, the full gravity of death. The preacher must name the pain, grief, agony, etc. for what it really is. Once it is named, we move to the second step: What does God have to say about the stark reality?

Step Two: Apply the Gospel to the Bad News

The preacher helps people to understand God's perspective on death. What is the word of the Lord unto the people that are experiencing this loss? What does the Bible say to this experience of grief and loss? What is the truth of God that will change perspective? The preacher applies the word of God to the tragic situation, and offers resolution that might take years to fully experience, but begins at the point of the funeral sermon.

Step Three: Celebrate the Gospel

The preacher celebrates the resolution of the bad news. The preacher affirms and joyfully reinforces God's resolution to the bad news. The preacher celebrates God's victory over death, and God's victory over death in this family's life. The preacher celebrates the power of God to comfort, heal, and overcome death.

Someone will probably say that this method is easy when the person is "saved" or is a believer in Christ. According to this line of thinking, if a person is a believer, then we know that he or she has the victory in Christ, but what about when a person is not saved, or has led a life that has offended some? I do not believe that it is our preaching task to put a person in hell. It is our task to offer the compassion, the mercy, and the love of God to the family. Most of the time, I will not mention the negative, or the embarrassing, or the shameful part of person's life at the funeral. Ultimately, I believe it is the preacher's task to offer the family hope, not by pretending that the person was a saint, but by the proclamation of a word from God that offers hope and healing. My focus is a healing word to the family from the word of God.

One of the best examples of the methodology that I set forth in this discussion is the account of a sermon entitled "Uncle Wash's Funeral."[4] It was found in slave narratives compiled in 1936. Ned Walker, a layperson, heard the sermon somewhere around 1866–67, and recounted it almost sixty years later:

> Now 'bout Uncle Wash's funeral. You know Uncle Wash was the blacksmith in the fork of the road, across the railroad from Concord church. He had been a mighty powerful man. He used the hammer and the tongs on behalf of all the people for miles and miles around.
>
> Uncle Wash joined the Springvale AME Church, but he kinda fell from grace, I guess. Somehow he was 'cused of stealing Marse Walter Brice's pig, and I guess he was guilty. At any rate, he was convicted and sent to the penitentiary. While he was down there, he contracted consumption and had to come home. His chest was all sunk in, and his ribs was full of rheumatism. He soon went to bed and died . . . .
>
> Uncle Pompey preached the funeral . . . and Uncle Pompey really knowed how to preach a funeral . . . Uncle Pompey took his text from that place in the Bible where Paul and Silas was a-layin' up in jail. He dwelt on Uncle Wash's life of hard work and bravery–how he tackled kickin' horses and mules, so's crops could be cultivated and harvested and hauled. He talked 'bout how he sharpened dull plow points to make the corn and the cotton grow, to feed the hungry and clothe the naked. He told what a good-hearted man Uncle Wash was, and then he 'llowed as how his goin' to jail did not necessarily mean he didn't go to heaven. He declared it wasn't eternally against a church member to get put in jail. If it hadda been, Paul and Silas wouldn't a made it to heaven, and he knowed they was there. In fact, they was lot a people in heaven what had been arrested.

Then he went to talkin' 'bout a vision of Jacob's ladder. "I see Jacob's ladder. An' I see Brother Wash. He's climbin' Jacob's ladder. Look like he's halfway up. I want y'all to pray with me that he enter the pearly gates, Brothers and Sisters. He's still a climbin'. I see the pearly gates. They is swingin' open. An' I see Brother Wash. He has done reached the topmost round of de ladder. Let us sing with all our hearts that blessed hymn, 'There Is a Fountain Filled with Blood.'"

When they sang the second verse, 'bout the dyin' thief rejoiced to see that fountain in his day, Uncle Pompey cried out over the crowd, "I see Brother Wash as he enters in, an' that dyin' thief is there to welcome him in. Thank God! Thank God! He's made it into Paradise. His sins has been washed away, an' he has landed safe forever more."

Well sir, I don't need to tell you that the women started to shout on the first verse, an' when they got to singing' 'bout the dying thief in heaven, *an' they seen the 'surance of grace that was in it, they like to never quit praisin' God* (emphasis mine).

Notes

[1]This article first appeared in Volume 4, Number 1, Winter 2000-2001 of *The African American Pulpit,* and is reprinted with the author's permission.
[2] Frank A. Thomas, *They Like To Never Quit Praisin' God: The Role of Celebration in Preaching* (Cleveland: United Church Press, 1997).
[3] Ibid., 31.
[4] This account was adapted from: *Born in Slavery: Slave Narratives from the Federal Writer's Project, 1936-1938, South Carolina Narratives,* Volume 14, Part 4, Narratives of Ned Walker ex-slave, 83 years-old. http://memory.loc.gov/cgi-bin/ampage?collId=mesn&fileName=144/mesn144.db&recNum=182&itemLink=S?ammem/mesnbib:@field(AUTHOR+@od1(Walker,+Ned))

Music in Africana Worship

MELINDA E. WEEKES

For Christian worshippers of the African Diaspora, music is the lifeblood of our communal experiences with God. From the moaned prayers of enslaved Africans, to the bouncing rhythms of church steel bands in the Caribbean, to the majesty of a senior choir's anthem, to a mouthful of rhymes put to hip-hop beats–our music is a central and centering means by which we encounter and revere God's presence.

In African culture, music is not just art to be admired; it is a practical tool of daily life. It may be part of a healing procedure, a tactic of warfare, or a conduit of tribal history. Similarly, in Africana worship, music is not only that which we offer to God as praise, it is foundational to how we navigate as a community once God's presence becomes manifest. We welcome and warm gathering parishioners with songs; an elder may spontaneously accent her testimonial with a beloved hymn; or we march our way around the church to the offering basket as a sign of cheerful giving. For a scattered people, the connecting role that music plays is particularly vital: it connects those assembled to the presence of God. It connects us to each other. It connects the socio-historical past to a present spirituality. And it helps weave the elements of a worship experience into a coherent, meaningful whole.

African culture plays a significant role in the ways music lives in the worship of people of African descent across the globe. For example, whether in Chicago, Carousal or Cape Town, black folks' ways of worshipping God entreat all assembled to participate. Music in the worship setting is not merely to be observed.[1] Nor is to be left to those who sing in the choir or who are professionally trained. Instead, our music, offered in worship, comes from within and flows throughout, *all* of the people–up to God.

Reflective of the tribal nature of African civil society, music in Africana worship is both communal and collaborative. The *call and response motif* replete throughout African culture, where there is an alternation between an individual and the group, is an example of a musical pattern present in Africana worship. It invites all those present into a community dialogue. Whether it is in the choral singing tradition of African Americans or in the Ghanaian "talking" drums that summon villagers to worship, African peoples employ music in worship in ways that transcend Western notions of separation between performer and audience. We are transformed from a gathering of many individuals, into a single worshipping community.

Music in Africana worship is not only participatory, it also is expressive. Africana worshippers exhibit outward signs of their inward feelings about God, whether with hand-clapping, congregational singing, ring-shouting, or tambourine playing. The deep pathos of the Negro spirituals, which sociologist W. E. B. Dubois referred to as "sorrow songs," displays this quality.[2] The fiesta-like energy from congregations in New York City, Venezuela and Puerto Rico that celebrate the power of God in coritos, or Latin-American praise songs, is another example.

In this highly participatory and expressive environment, a third distinction of Africana worship emerges: improvisation. Improvisation may appear in many musical forms, all of which reinforce the immediacy of God's presence in the midst of the assembly. A soloist may create lyrics on the spot to testify of a current personal situation known to the congregation; a parishioner may break out in a shout and dance to display an unspeakable joy; an organist may add musical color to a composition that was not accounted for in the sheet music to depict an emotion resonate within the congregation.[3] In these and countless other ways, Africana worshippers employ spontaneity not just as a cultural, but also as a liturgical, resource in such a way that communal senses and sensibilities are heightened to the presence of God. Africana worshippers are mindful of the fact that we worship an ever-present God that is indeed with us continually–in new, relevant, and dynamic ways.

The customs, traditions and styles of worship of the African Diaspora reflect diversity as magnificent as the length and breadth of the Diaspora itself.

These musical expressions give us a small, but important, glimpse of one of the many contributions of Africana Christian worshippers to Christendom. Every Sunday, and each day in between, we offer our music in worship to God, as praise for the God who has championed our cause, faithfully sustained us and who continues to lead and love us–as individuals and as a people. Our musical worship reflects our conviction that, as a people, we were indeed created to make God's praise glorious. With music–and everything else that is beautiful within our grasp–we do worship Christ!

Notes

[1] Wendell P. Whalum, Black Hymnody, Review and Expositor, 1973,Volume LXX, No. 3.
[2] DuBois, William Edward Burghardt, *The Souls of Black Folk* (New York: Vintage Books, 1990).
[3] Patricia K. Maultsy, The Use and Performance of Hymnody, Spirituals, and Gospels in the Black Church, The Papers of the Hymn Society, 1983.

Doxology in Darkness[1]

JESSICA KENDALL INGRAM

My God, My God, why have you forsaken me?
Why are you so far from helping me?
And from the words of my groaning?

O my God, I cry in the daytime, but you do not hear
And in the night season and am not silent.

Psalm 22:1-2 (NKJV)

Now to Him who is able to do exceedingly abundantly
More than we can ask or think according to the power
That works in us; To him be glory in the church
By Christ forever and ever. Amen

Ephesians 3:20-21 (NKJV)

This ministry God has given to us, this calling on our lives, requires us to have the ability to learn to live with the existential reality that we engage in ministry while we cope with, adjust to, deal with, and accept the polarities, the opposites, the paradoxes that are non-negotiable dimensions of what we do.

This ministry we have is full of polarities, contradictions, and paradoxes. In this ministry, we have moments of great joy and days of great pain. We have times of amazing clarity when we can see clearly what God wants us to do and then we have times of great confusion when we don't have a clue as to what to do. We have those times when we speak and it happens immediately and there are those times when we speak it and we wait and wait and wait and nothing happens. We know what it means to be highly honored and despised at the same time; to be surrounded by a crowd of people and yet feel very much alone; to have great financial gain, but also experience great financial losses. It is an experience of having the ability through our preaching and teaching to effectively transform the lives of others and yet our lives are falling completely apart. Did I say this ministry we have is an experience of learning to live with the polarities of our calling?

We have high mountain experiences and then we descend into the valley of despair. Sometimes we pray and it is done before we get up from our knees and at other times we pray and our prayers just ricochet back to us from the wall and they go nowhere. Yes, we experience seasons of spiritual consolation, when we are spiritually in tune, where we know for sure that we know God and that God knows us. But then we go through seasons of great spiritual desolation. It is what St. John of the Cross describes as the "dark night of the soul." It is what the Psalmist was experiencing when he said, "My God why have you forsaken me? It is the night season of my life and I can't hear a word from you." I like the way Eugene Peterson expresses these verses in *The Message* Bible when he says, "God, God . . . my God! Why did you dump me miles from nowhere? Doubled up with pain, I call to God all the day long. No answer. Nothing. I keep at it all night, tossing and turning. And you! Are you indifferent, above it all, leaning back on the cushions of Israel's praise?" (The Message, Psalm 22:1-3).

The Psalmist knew what it meant to experience the nearness of God. God had been so very present to him, he could feel God's breathe on his face. God had surrounded him with his glory, anointed his head with oil such that there was an overflow. God put a new song in his mouth; every time he spoke, something new and wonderful came forth. He had known a time when God had heard his cry and immediately dispatched angels to minister to his wounds. God was so close but now it is the night season in his life; now it is midnight; now daily he wakes up to a brooding cloud that hovers over him; now it is pitch black in his life; now darkness has overcome him and he cannot hear a word from God. And so he cries:

> My God, my God why hast thou forsaken me (KJV)? Why, why, why are you so far from me? I answered you when you called me, God; I said yes to your will and yes to you way. Why, God, are you acting like you don't hear me calling to you now? I have done your work. I have being faithful to the assignment. I have made great sacrifices. I have given up much. I have given up my job, relocated, gone to school with my old self, took the little church that they gave me, put myself under authority, coped with being single and in ministry, dealt with being married and in ministry, struggled with my mother moments and being in ministry, suffered through the attacks, the slander, the gossip, the stuff that goes with ministry. And now that I need you for this one thing I desperately need I can't hear from you and this darkness has descended upon my life! –Yet I still must do what you have called me to do. I feel like I am dying and yet I must continue to speak life to others.

It is a paradox. (I think that there are about fifty of you here this evening that can identify with the psalmist's predicament. You know what it means to be in your season of spiritual desolation and you can't hear anything from God for your situation).

My sisters, can I tell you this: the people we are ministering to don't know what we are going through because we have mastered our public ministry *persona*, which is different from our private spiritual realities. It is the paradox of our ministry: got a word for the people, get up and preach like a crazy woman and then go back to our hotel rooms, get in the bed, pull the covers all the way over our head and cry ourselves to sleep. (Does anybody know what I am talking about?)

How do we keep doing what we do while in our night seasons when we don't hear from God? How do we tell others God will answer their prayers and seemingly God is not answering ours? How do we keep preparing sermons where we hear from God a word to give others but we can't hear anything for our own personal needs? How do we keep doing the work, engaging in the tenets of ministry for God when God acts like what we are doing does not matter? How do we keep talking to a God who will not talk to us?

Mother Teresa once wrote these words: "Jesus has a very special love for you. But as for me, the silence and the emptiness is so great that I look and do not see, listen and do not hear."[2] Talk about a private spiritual reality different from her public persona. Here Mother Teresa was doing the work, had an international reputation as one who sacrificed it all, pictures of her exuded the presence of a humble woman who had a deep and abiding relationship with God.

That was her public persona. But her private reality was this: In letters she wrote that during the last fifty years of her life she did not feel the presence of God; she existed in an arid landscape from which God had disappeared and where she felt no presence of God whatsoever. In her letters she says:

> Lord my God, who am I that you should forsake me? The child of your love and now become the most hated one–the one you have thrown away as unwanted, unloved. I call, I cling, I want and there is no One to answer. . . . I am told God loves me and yet the reality of darkness and coldness and emptiness is so great that nothing touches my soul. Did I make a mistake in surrendering blindly to the call of the sacred heart? . . . If this brings you glory, if souls are brought to you, with joy I accept it all.[3]

Mother Teresa had whispered a doxology in the midst of her darkness.

Can you identify with Mother Teresa? I know I can because this past year, since this exact time last year, I have had to learn to live with the polarities of my life: doing a great work in the Tenth Episcopal District of the African Methodist Episcopal Church in Texas, while at the same time I was in the midst of the greatest pain I have ever experienced in my life; leading people in praising God, encouraging them to put glad hands together and give God praise and then going home and literally crying all night long; teaching people intimacy with God, telling them to have consistent daily set aside time with God and how in so doing God would be so very near to them and yet morning, after morning, after morning, I went to my prayer chair, to my quiet time space, and no matter how many books I read, no matter how much I wrote in my journal, no matter how long I stayed on my knees, I am telling you that for month after month after month I did not hear a thing from God. I prayed the same prayer over and over again and got absolutely no response. I am talking about my private spiritual reality that was different from my public persona. I led women in Texas to new places in God while I slipped into a deep, deep dark hole where I could not see the light of day. Can I identify with the words of Mother Teresa? Yes, I can.

So I begin to ask God: what am I experiencing? What is it called? What is the purpose of it? What am I suppose to learn from it? I feel like I have been duped. I have given so much in ministry, sacrificed so much and this how you repay me? And I am here to tell you that slowly but surely God began to open my understanding and let me know that he permits polarities in our lives –the opposites if you would–because God does his best work when we are on the downside. God does his best work when we experience the midnights of our soul. It is in darkness that we learn more about God than we do in the light. It is when we are in the valley that we see God differently from when we are on the mountaintop. It is when we are going through that we experience him differently from when we come out. It is when we feel alone that we can better appreciate God's nearness. It is when we don't hear from God that we learn to value his speaking.

God permits darkness to descend upon our lives because it is here we learn how to depend totally on him. Hear me now! Sometimes God has to strip us of both our exterior and interior spiritual dependencies. Exterior spiritual dependencies: what we tend to do is define the legitimacy of our spiritual life based upon the number of ecstatic moments we have with God. We measure our ministry by this exterior manifestation of God's presence in our lives. Listen to me. This time is a dangerous spiritual season in the church's life, for more and more there are those who are establishing spiritual measuring rods based upon how often they are taken up to the third heaven; how often they have great spiritual experience; how often they hear from God.

I have had to deal with my own sense of spiritual guilt. I have felt that something was wrong with me when I am around those ministers who are always on fire; always got a word; always got a direct word from God; always know exactly what God has said. And here I am at my lowest point. Here I am having prayed for family members to live and they die anyway. Here I am feeling like I have been duped–after all these years, twenty-five years of consistently coming before God in the morning, writing in my journal, reading every spiritual writer that you can think of, delving into the word, getting on my knees, lying stretched out on the floor, and after all these years I am at a place where I can't hear from God. I felt like God had taken a sabbatical from me. And I felt so awkward around these always deep-spiritual-hearing-from-God-all-the-time preachers until I came to realize they are just lying. Lying. They are in denial, and they are just afraid, ashamed to get up and admit: "Looka' here, I ain't heard nothing from God this week. As a matter of fact, I ain't heard from God this year, but I am going to preach based upon what I already know, what I have already experienced, what I have already heard from God." None of us hear from God all the time. And when we don't hear God's voice, listen to me, God is speaking to us in the silence. Silence is God's way of getting us to pay closer attention to him. You see, preachers, we can become so programmed and so accustomed to experiencing God in prescribed ways until we begin to take God for granted. But we cannot limit and define how God will show up. God's silence in the midst of our darkness is his way of teaching us to perceive him in new ways and in new places.

In her book titled *Listening for God*,[4] Dr. Renita Weems says when she found herself in the midst of her silence, she had to learn to stop peeping behind altars and looking for epiphanies but to allow the lull between those moments to become an opportunity to seek God in new ways. In other words, my sisters, don't grow so accustomed to hearing God in loud praise in the sanctuary, or in the vibrating moment of preaching, so accustomed to our way of worship, so accustomed to prescribed ways of praying until we don't look for God or expect God to come in other way. We can't limit how God will manifest.

One of the ways God strips us of interior results is to allow us to live in spiritual darkness. Interior stripping, you see, is even more painful because it threatens us at the root of all we believe in and all we've given ourselves to. Paradoxically, God is purifying our faith by threatening to destroy it. God's silence during our midnights produces barrenness in our soul and allows us to look at what is superficial and false within us. We are being taken off of vain securities and false allegiances. In God's silence we learn detachment, humility, patience, and perseverance. It is here in darkness we learn ruthless trust. It is here we learn to seek God until we find him, to pray not so much until we get an answer, but to pray until we can trust God no matter what.

When our lives are no longer in working order and we face strange crises, and we find that we cannot live the afternoon of our lives according to the morning program; when failure and rejection, abandonment and betrayal, loneliness and depression, sickness and the loss of loved ones, when cosmic disorder and systemic evil enters our lives and our sunshiny days turn into midnight, it is here that we learn how to praise God in the darkness–that's our doxology. For a doxology is a declaration of praise to God, expressing his power and glory. And we can't understand God's power and glory until we have experienced darkness.

So when you are going through great trial and tribulation; when you are going through great pain and pathos; when you are experiencing aloneness and loneliness; when you have been through disappointments and defeats; when you have great sadness and setbacks, hurt and heartache, abandonment and abuse; when the saints are acting like ain'ts; when ministry becomes more than what you think you can bear; and when you too come to the place where the psalmist was and you cry out *My God, My God why hast thou forsaken me* and even if you don't feel God's presence right now, and even if God doesn't answer you right now, I am here to tell you that you can still say a doxology in the midst of your present darkness. Why? Because you have a memory, because you are not suffering from spiritual amnesia and because you can remember what God has done for you in the past and your spiritual memory clicks in.

Click, click. You remember what God has already brought you through when you thought you could not make it. Click, click. You remember how he already made a way out of no way. Click, click. You remember how God already opened doors people shut. Click, click: how God already made your enemy your footstool, how he already fought your battle. Click, click: how he already wiped the tears from your eyes, how your weeping lasted for the night, but joy did come in the morning. Chick, click. You remember how God already gave you strength while you waited and you mounted up on the wings of an eagle and you ran and did not get weary, how you walked and did not faint.

And so now, although it may be darker than a thousand midnights in your life, you can whisper a doxology because through the process of God's absence you have come to know that God is very present. You can whisper a doxology in darkness because your past experience with God has taught you that your situation and the longevity of it do not change God's essential nature. He is still the same God. You can say a doxology in the midst of what you are going through because as you grow in grace and knowledge you come to understand that God's timing is different from yours, but God knows what time to come through.

And so in the midst of your night season, in the midst of your midnights, in the midst of your darkness you can say with confidence and boldness:

> Glory to God in the highest (Luke 2:14); For Thine is the kingdom and the power and the glory forever and forever and ever. Amen (Matthew 6:13); Thine is the greatness and the power and the glory and the victory and the majesty for all that is in heaven and in the earth is Thine; Thine is the kingdom O Lord and thou art exalted as head above (1 Chronicles 29:11); Blessed be the God of Israel from everlasting to everlasting. Amen (Psalm 41:13). Blessed be the Lord God, the God of Israel who only doeth wondrous things and blessed be his glorious name forever and ever (Psalm 72:18).

And so even in those moments when you don't hear God's voice, don't feel his presence, don't have an answer to your prayer, you can say:

> Now unto him who is able *(yes he is still able. The fact that my situation has not changed does not mean that he is not able; he is able; just because I am still going through does not mean God cannot bring me through; he is still able to regulate my mind, fix my broken heart, bind up my wounds, lift up my bowed down head, give me strength for the journey)*–Now unto him who is able to do exceedingly abundantly above all that I can ask or thing according to the power that worketh in me, unto him be the glory in the church *(in my life, in my ministry)* throughout all of the ages, world without end (Ephesians 3:20-21, paraphrased). Amen. **Amen.**

Notes

[1] *This is the edited version of a sermon preached for the 2007 Women in Ministry Conference, Atlanta, Georgia, in September 2007, convened by Rev. Dr. Cynthia Hale et al and the Ray of Hope Christian Church (Disciples of Christ).*
[2] Excerpt from a letter written in 1979 to her spiritual confidant, the Rev. Michael van der Peet and included in a book detailing letters and conversations over a 66-year period, *Mother Teresa: Come Be My Light* (Doubleday), as reported by David van Biema, "Her Agony," in *Time* vol. 170, no. 10 (September 03, 2007), 36-43.
[3] Ibid.
[4] Renita Weems, *Listening for God: A Minister's Journey through Silence and Doubt* (New York: Touchstone, a division of Simon & Schuster, 2000).

In the Spirit

Lisa Allen

What is worship? What does it mean? And when we add the descriptor, *black* what is unique about that? Edwin Womack, the author of *Come, Follow Me*,[1] states that worship is the most important thing we do. Indeed, worship comes from an old Anglo-Saxon word–*woerthan,* which meant *to declare how much something was worth.* Second, worship is action. The Greek New Testament uses several words translated into English as worship. Notice that they are all verbs–action words. The first word is *sebomai,* which means *to lift up or exalt.* In Christian worship it means recognizing God as highest, as greatest, giving God the glory and honor God deserves. The literal meaning of the second word, *proskuneo,* usually translated bow down, is *to kiss forward.* In ancient times, when a person would come before the king, she or he would literally bow down, with hands, feet, and forehead to the ground. In this position of subservience the person could not fight and was completely helpless. We show this kind of complete submission when we bow down before God. The third word, *latreuo,* means *to serve.* The word calls to remembrance the hired servant who gives faithful service to her master in return for the food, shelter, and money, which make it possible to live.

Don Saliers asserts that the continued worship of God in the assembly is a form of theology.[2] He calls this *primary theology.* If we use Daniel Migliore's definition of theology, *fides quarem intellectum,* faith seeking understanding[3], then worship is the believer (one who has faith) engaging in acts that seek to know (to sense, to experience, to understand) the One in whom belief is held.

What, then, is black Christian worship? What makes it unique? Is it not like all other Christian worship–acts of faith seeking understanding? Yes, it is that, and more. It is worship that pays attention to the historical location of those worshipping, the shared experiences of those who came out the wil'deness leaning on the Lord; it is the faithful utterance of those who couldn't hear nobody pray, those who felt like motherless children because nobody knew the trouble they'd seen–all while remembering that there is a Balm in Gilead! These and more make the black worship experience not just faith seeking understanding, but faith seeking freedom!

According to Dr. Melva Costen, African American Christians share several common aspects of worship regardless of denomination: 1) gathering to offer thanks and praise to God in and through Jesus Christ, and to be spiritually fed by the Word of God; 2) a common historical taproot, extending deep into the African soil; and 3) our history of struggle for survival as African people in America.[4]

The similarities in black churches that transcend denominational boundaries should come as no surprise given the context in which Christianity took root in the communities of enslaved Africans. E. Franklin Frazier coined the term *invisible institution* to describe the earliest slave initiation into Christianity.[5] As an act of both faith and defiance, enslaved Africans held their own secret church meetings, where they would not have to ascribe to the *white man's god* or labels of inferiority. In these secret meetings, blended aspects of their African heritage and belief systems were merged with the Christian worship experiences offered by their captors. The daily experiences of the enslaved led them to develop a holistic religious consciousness that included all they had seen and heard, past and present, good and bad. Thus, an Africanized Christianity was born, "a unique interaction between the white . . . world view and the black African/American world view, resulting in a new black . . . Sacred Cosmos."[6]

Dr. Robert Franklin tells us that the worship experience for enslaved persons was *multisensory.* In his book, *Another Day's Journey,* he states, "Given the difficulty and dehumanizing nature of their work, slaves created sacred space as a zone of ultimate freedom. In worship, the mind, emotions, and other sensory capacities were engaged in transcending the banality of evil."[7] For the enslaved, worship was a time of liberation, when they could praise the Creator for sparing them one more day, a day closer to freedom, either in this life or the next. This led to a worship experience that transcended the horrific consequences of their lives and subsequently, gave many a will to live, to "run on and see what the end's gon' be."

So, then, a black theology of worship holds that all of life is sacred, that worship occurs in all of everyday living. As black people, the realities with which we deal daily–the oppression and injustices of racism, sexism, classism–do not hinder us from having faith in God. Rather, our faith allows us to worship God in and through this daily reality because we understand that worship is also an eschatological event. We believe that the God who delivered the enslaved out of Egypt is the same God who delivered the enslaved out of Georgia, is the same God who broke through history in the person of Jesus Christ, and is the same God who breaks through history to deliver us. We know that God is a God of justice and liberation who does not leave God's people comfortless and promises to save and to restore humanity to the kingdom of God. And so we worship!

How do we worship? We worship through prayer, praise, and the preached Word. Let us discuss prayer first. I would suggest that African Americans incorporate prayer in worship in the forms of invocations, the deacon's prayer, altar calls, prayers by the pastor or other clergy, and benedictions. According to John Mbiti, "invocations show a spontaneous response to God, asking God to intervene for a particular purpose. They show that people consider God to be ever close to them, ready to respond to their need, and not subject to religious formalities."[8] The deacon's prayer tends to follow a pattern, "in which many of the attitudes toward God and the present world-order are recurrent."[9] In other words, the traditional prayers offered by deacons in some black church settings remind us who we are and from whence we have come. Their prayers remind us that God is Omnipotent, Omniscient, and Omnipresent and that God is present in the Church. It is this God who has '"brought us from a mighty long way." The altar call meets the needs of worshipers who are seeking special prayer, healing, or blessing.[10] During the altar call, worshippers have an opportunity to physically approach God with their problems and often their despair, and to issue a personal invitation for God to be present and active in their affairs. The benediction invites the congregation to leave united, *on one accord,* and sends them forth to serve as God's witnesses to a lost and dying world. These prayers are part of the theological act of worship, for in them we approach the throne of grace with holy boldness, seeking to know what we understand of God's will for our lives, and trusting God to handle that which we neither understand nor can change. These prayers take forms that come from African ways of approaching, experiencing, and responding to God.

Like other aspects of African American worship, black preaching grew out of an inherently African worldview about God and life. Sacred speech, in African traditional religious observances included ecstatic dancing and singing, "working up the spirit" until the oracle would go into a trance, be descended upon by divinity, and speak what was given her/him by the divinity. Parallels can be seen in African American Christian worship where the preacher's inspiration to speak comes from the Holy Spirit and the sacred speech, or *sermon*, is often preceded by ecstatic singing and praise. The dialogical or characteristic *call and response* delivery style of many black sermons also finds its roots in African culture. Dr. Henry Mitchell says this about black preaching style: "The black style, which includes the pattern of call and response, is very easily traceable to black African culture. Black preaching has had an audience from the beginning."[11]

Genres of music particular to the African American church are *the shout* (music that accompanies an ecstatic dance done to the cadence of favorite shout songs or running spirituals), *the Spiritual*, which has been called the first authentic American folk song form and expressed religious fervor related to situations of struggle, *lined or metered hymns*, *hymns by African American composers*, and *gospel* music. This rich musical heritage is heavily influenced by African rhythms and chants. Skilled present-day organists and instrumentalists remind us of the continued African practice of using drumbeats as a form of symbolic speech. Music becomes a worship dialogue where God speaks and believers respond in praise. Indeed, one well-known African proverb states, "The Spirit cannot descend without a song." Music alone can serve as invocation, prayer, praise, or the Word in song. As Dr. Costen has asserted, music is not merely a means of expressing feelings. It evokes the reciprocal activity of imagination and understanding of the soul. The sound of music born of human breath bore witness to the presence and love of God in the being of black folks from the beginning of time.[12]

Now, what is the significance of all this? How do we respond to the rich heritage of African American worship in this day and time of public access television and mega-church polity where worship is being approached from a *lights, camera, action* perspective (to paraphrase Dr. James Abbington).[13] In many churches, there is no longer any *lining out* of hymns, lifting a cappella spirituals during the prayer or even rocking to Mahalia's "How I Got Over." Again I quote Dr. Abbington, "A successful worship service in many churches is measured by the fact that the pastor and the choir stirred up frenzy on Sunday morning and the people were glad. Whether or not the members of the congregation can recall the sermon title or text is not important as long as they got their shout on."[14]

Please do not misunderstand me. I am not against contemporary worship. I am speaking of how worship is merely entertainment in some local contexts and, moreover, how worship planning is not being done or is being done without theological, historical, or liturgical underpinnings, many times by students with seminary educations!

Historically, worship in the black Church, as we have described it, has been about acknowledging and praising the Almighty God for God's saving acts, lifting up the name of Jesus, confessing our sins, celebrating the sacraments, and going forth to serve humanity. The focus was on God, not on us! Worship was about being together in community, sharing concerns and celebrations, being in the presence of God–not about being entertained!

Worship is not meant to follow an entertainment model, even if it gets people in the doors, and/or gets people to join. Why? Because that type of worship is usually more style than substance, often consisting of a hodgepodge of disparate elements that have nothing to do with one another.

Worship planning entails a collaborative effort of those who know, not only the elements of worship and how they fit together, but also the historical, theological and liturgical foundations of worship and how best to utilize them from Sunday to Sunday. Worship is never for entertainment purposes, but rather for a meaningful, substantive encounter with God that engages the worshipper in a potentially transformative experience. This is why training and preparation are so important. Seminary students must be formed in these liturgical practices if they are to be able to refer to them and use them to develop worthwhile models of worship.

Do we understand and can we articulate what is liturgical, theological, and historically authentic about our prayers, our praise, our preaching and the ways that we celebrate the sacraments *and* can we use this knowledge to plan authentic black worship? Is our worship formed out of immediacy, the latest cultural idea or program, or is it a continuation of our historical legacy that holds all of life as sacred? If a theology of worship holds all of life as sacred and exalts God as a God of justice and liberation, recalls what God has done for us through more than 400 years of oppression and also through last week, and has hope as its foundation, then that is a theology around which we can build a worship service that has meaning and substance in the black church. From this theology, we can build worship that acknowledges the changing culture, but does not lose the deep sigh of our ancestors. *Ashe.*

Bibliography

Abbington, James. *Let Mount Zion Rejoice: Music in the African American Church,* Judson Press, 2001.

Cone, James. *A Black Theology of Liberation.* Philadelphia: J. B. Lippincott Company, 1970.

Costen, Melva. *African American Christian Worship.* Nashville: Abingdon Press, 1993.

Franklin, Robert. *Another Day's Journey.* Minneapolis: Fortress Press, 1997.

Frazier, E. Franklin. *The Negro Church in America.* Liverpool: The University of Liverpool, 1963.

Hamilton, Charles. *The Black Preacher in America.* New York: William Morrow &Company, Inc., 1972.

Johnson-Smith, Robert, Ed. Wisdom of the Ages: *The Mystique of the African American Preacher.* Valley Forge: Judson Press, 1995.

Lincoln, C. Eric, and Lawrence Mamiya. *The Black Church in the African American Experience.* Durham: Duke University Press, 1996.

Mays, Benjamin, and Joseph Nicholson. *The Negro's Church.* New York: The Institute of Social and Religious Research, 1969.

Mbiti, John. *African Religions and Philosophy,* 2d Ed. Portsmouth, New Hampshire: Heinemann Educational Publishers, 1999.

McClain, William. "What is Authentic Black Worship?" In *Experiences, Struggles, and Hopes of the Black Church,* ed. James Gadsden, 69-84. Nashville: Discipleship Resources-Tidings, 1975.

Migliore, Daniel. *Faith Seeking Understanding: An Introduction to Christian Theology.* Wm. B. Eerdmans Publishing Co., 1991.

Mitchell, Henry. *Black Preaching.* New York: J. B. Lippincott Company, 1970.

Roberts, J. Deotis. *The Prophethood of Black Believers.* Louisville, Kentucky: Westminster/John Knox Press, 1994.

_____________. *Roots of a Black Future: Family and Church.* Philadelphia: The Westminster Press, 1980.

Saliers, Don. *Worship as Theology.* Abingdon Press, 1994.

Sobel, Mechal. *Trabelin' On: The Slave Journey to an Afro-Baptist Faith.* Westport, Connecticut: Greenwood Press, 1979.

Washington, Joseph. *Black Religion.* Boston: Beacon Press, 1974.

Watley, William. *Singing the Lord's Song in a Strange Land.* Geneva, Switzerland: WCC Publications, World Council of Churches, 1993.

Womack, Edwin. *Come, Follow Me: A Study Book for Acolytes.* CSS Publishing, 2004.

Notes

[1] Edwin Womack, *Come Follow Me: A Study Book for Acolytes* (CSS Publishing, 2004).

[2] Don Saliers, *Worship as Theology* (Abingdon Press, 1994).

[3] Daniel Migliore, *Faith Seeking Understanding: An Introduction to Christian Theology,* Eerdmans, 1991.

[4] Melva Costen, *African American Christian Worship* (Abingdon, 1993), 13-14.

[5] E. Franklin Frazier, *The Negro Church in America* (The University of Liverpool, 1963).
[6] Mechal Sobel, *Trabelin' On: The Slave Journey to an Afro-Baptist Faith* (Westport, Connecticut: Greenwood Press, 1979), 80.
[7] Robert Franklin, *Another Day's Journey* (Fortress Press, 1997), 30.
[8] John Mbiti, *African Religions and Philosophy,* 2nd Edition (Portsmouth, NH: Heinemann Educational Publishers, 1999), 65.
[9] Benjamin Mays and Joseph Nicholsen, *The Negro's Church* (New York: The Institute of Social and Religious Research, 1969), 145.
[10] Costen, 108.
[11] Henry Mitchell, *Black Preaching* (New York: J. B. Lippincott Company, 1970), 47.
[12] Costen, 44.
[13] James Abbington, *Let Mount Zion Rejoice: Music in the African American Church* (Judson, 2001).
[14] Ibid., 50.

That Was Then, This Is NOW[1]

Otis B. Moss III

Joshua son of Nun was full of the spirit of wisdom, because Moses had laid his hands on him; and the Israelites obeyed him, doing as the Lord had commanded Moses (Deuteronomy 34:9, NRSV).

The boy in M. Knight Shyamalan's movie *The Sixth Sense* makes a statement that has been canonized within the pop culture lexicon of America. That statement is "I see dead people." And, beloved, I see *dead churches.* Dead to the fact that it's 2005 and not 1955. Dead and unable to engage critical issues for an unchurched generation. Dead to the fact that *three points, a poem,* and *a whoop* are not enough to demand the attention of a Joshua generation. Dead–still using antiquated theological constructs, outdated doctrinal mortise, irrelevant tradition, romanticized liturgical forms to reach a postmodern, post-soul, post-civil rights, virtual-equipped generation.

Worse yet, dead to the new reality that the stalwart institution we call the church is in danger of losing its power because urban poetics we call rappers carry more weight and influence with our youth than any preacher, apostle, elder, or bishop.

You see there is a paradigm shift moving across the ecclesiastical landscape of America. If we miss the shift, our churches will be nothing more than boasting apparitions of what could have been and should have been. That thing you were holding on to–that was then, but God is doing something in the now.

The scripture text offers a glimpse at how God deals with the generation gap. The thirty-fourth chapter of Deuteronomy recounts the home-going of Moses. The mourning, the sorrow, the reverence are clearly illustrated in Deuteronomy 34. The patriot is canonized in Hebraic literature as a hero of the people and all Israel mourns. That was then.

But, when you move to Joshua 1, this is now. We see in verse 1–2 God's desire to make sure the people are not paralyzed by their past or stuck in their sorrow. The text says: "Moses is dead." Let me say it again for those who are maybe vanguards of tradition and have mythologized their yesterdays. *Moses is dead!* No longer will the great patriarchy of Hebraic liberation dispense wisdom transmitted from the illusive but ever-present God of salvation whose very utterance ignited a divine creative spark that caused time to start ticking.

Moses is dead. The progenitor of liberation theology and the originator of clinical pastoral education would no longer chair the church meetings when Assistant Pastor Aaron was trying to split the congregation.

Moses is dead. No more wandering in the wilderness, living in makeshift homes, in shotgun houses, eating manna from heaven, and drinking water from rocks.

Moses is dead. The songs of the previous generation will no longer be sung, for the saints who used to sing these tunes used to pass them from mouth unto ear. But, a new generation is going to sample the old and make a remix for this generation.

Moses is dead. The ideological call and response rooted in the Southern vernacular of moans and amen will be replaced by urban inspired praise peppered with neo-African Pentecostal flavor with a hip-hop vibe.

Moses is dead. No longer can the high priest of yesteryear's ministries assume biblical or canonical literacy for their congregation. They didn't experience slavery. They don't know Jim Crow. They don't know segregation. They don't know Emmett Till. They don't know about four little girls being bombed in Alabama. They don't know so they need somebody who understands a new methodology that can bring them into the future. Moses is dead!

Even going to the tabernacle dressed to the nines is a faded memory because a portion of this generation has long paper and major cheddar, and another segment of this population is trying to make a dollar out of fifteen cents.

They will come to the tabernacle with Phat Farm and Sean John because the ascetic principle of fashion has shifted from Brooks Brothers to Roc-a-Fella.

Moses is now dead. It's a different ministry in a post-Moses generation. The church, if she is to reclaim her primacy among the dispossessed young and young adults and those who are unchurched, must recognize these shifts.

And, we are now living in a post-soul generation. You see, prior to the 1960s the black church was the epicenter of all cultural, social, and political activity. It was a soul culture. You see, all musical forms except hip-hop come out of the vernacular of the faith-based community we call the church. If you talk about spirituals, blues, jazz, R&B, and gospel, it all comes from the church.

You see, before Marvin Gaye could sing "What's Going On?" he was influenced by a Pentecostal father and pastor. Before Aretha Franklin sang "Respect," she was singing "Amazing Grace" under the tutelage of her father, C. L. Franklin. Before Sam Cook sang "You Send Me," he was singing with the Highway QCs. But you see, when you talk about T.I., Lil' Kim, and 50 Cent–they are post-soul. They don't know what you're talking about. They're not from the same vernacular that you're from.

See, some of y'all think that hip-hop started ten years ago or maybe fifteen or twenty years. But, I'm here to tell you that it started more than twenty years ago. You see, in 1972 in the South Bronx, there was a brother by the name of Kool DJ Herc. Herc didn't have enough money to buy a guitar, but he had two turntables and a microphone to get the party started. He became an urban griot that was letting people in other parts of the South Bronx know what was happening in the community.

So from 1972 to 1978, hip-hop was an underground phenomenon, especially in places like New York, Chicago, and L.A. But, in 1978 things changed when Sugarhill Gang came out with "Rapper's Delight." Hip-hop was on the national scene, but it was still owned and operated in the black community. But, in 1983 while Reaganomics was destroying our community and black unemployment among youth was seventy percent in New York, a group decided to critique Reaganomics in the urban environment. This group was called Grand Master Flash and The Furious Five. And so, the message came out in 1983.

But hold up–wait a minute. Things began to shift. In 1985 gangsta rap was born. Corporations–Time Warner, AOL, Song–realized they could make money off of this music, and so they bought all the independent labels that were owned by us and then signed contracts with young men between the ages of fourteen and twenty-two and said: "If you want to sell your records nationally, you've got to call sisters out of their name. If you want to sell your records nationally, you've got to say the 'N' word so many times." So, *gangsta rap* was born in the streets, but it was nursed upon the breasts of corporate America.

But, wait a minute. This thing messes me up because as gangsta rap was born, crack hit the street in every urban community. Now, I'm not a conspiracy theorist, but it's mighty strange that we've got gangsta rap on one hand and crack on the other hand. But then simultaneously as this is happening in the '70s, we have the death of public space. What are you talking about?

Well, architecture shifted in America because at first, during and up until 1962, when you designed your home you put a front porch on it. And, many of us are from households and communities that believe in front porch theology. Y'all know what front porch theology is? It's when you stand on the front porch and you're watching all the children in the community. But during the '70s we shifted from the front porch to create back porches with privacy fences–living in suburban cul-de-sac communities where you no longer knew your neighbors. So, therefore, your children could act crazy and you wouldn't even have another village member to bring them back to center.

But, as this was happening, we then had the rise of Wal-Mart, which is destroying unions and creating a de-industrialized urban landscape. And as jobs move out, gangs move in. As jobs move out, then drugs move in. So, all of this is happening and what is the church doing? We're arguing whether we should sing this hymn or sing this anthem. We're arguing about if it's all right to praise God. Don't stand up; it doesn't take all of that. Meanwhile, our children are going to hell in a handbasket.

But, watch this now. The principle is that you cannot use a Moses methodology on a Joshua generation. We get so caught up on the method that we miss out on the message. We should focus on message and not on methodology. Let me break it down this way. How many people here grew up listening to music on a 78? Y'all know about a 78? Anybody in here know about a 33? Anybody in here know about a 45? You carried your spindle to the party. Anybody here know about an 8-track tape? Anybody here know about an LP? A cassette? A CD? A DVD? An MP3? But, guess what. You see, I can play the song "Amazing Grace" on a 78, a 33, a 45, an 8-track, an LP, a cassette, a CD, a DVD, an MP3–it's the same song, but a different method of delivery.

The problem with some of our churches is we've got 8-track churches in a CD world. And you're wondering why you can't reach this generation.

Some of us are so caught up on the method that we miss out on the message. You see, you can use the pillars of hip-hop to help transmit new values to this generation. Say, wait a minute. What are the pillars of hip-hop, Moss?

Well, there are four pillars to hip-hop: graffiti, DJ-ing, rapping, and movement. You see each pillar has a universal connection. Graffiti is nothing but art. You've got art in the church, and you have a generation that wants to express itself artistically. Second is DJ-ing–the universal axiom is technology. You have a generation that is not technophobic. Stop putting folk over the sound ministry that don't know how to use the stuff in the first place. Put somebody who understands the technology!

Maybe you're saying, I ain't going to have no rapping up in the church. Well, rapping–the universal axiom of it–is orality. You see, within the African vernacular we believe in the oral transmission of information. So, if you would use poetry and rhyming, you can help this generation understand how they can use their verbal skills to rise to the level that God wants them to rise.

Then there's movement–break dancing. Break dancing is nothing but movement. Ah, if the Lord can tell David, "Dance with all your might," then maybe we need some movement in the church! As Ludacris would say, "When I move, you move!"

And so we have these pillars of hip-hop. Now, the interesting thing is that Joshua is not a Moses clone. Y'all missed it! God is about to do a remix with Joshua. Joshua will sample from Moses, but then he will remix it into something new.

And so, Moses says you can sample from me and do a remix for your generation. You see, my greatest DJ is Jesus because Jesus knows how to remix. Y'all missed it. When Jesus was in the wilderness and said, "Man does not live on bread alone,"[2] that's a remix from the Torah. When Jesus gave his inaugural sermon, "The Spirit of the Lord is upon me,"[3] it's a remix from Isaiah. When Jesus said, "You have heard it said love your neighbor and hate your enemies"–hold up! Here's the remix: "But I tell you, love your enemies and pray for those who persecute you."[4] A remix is nothing but the same song with a different beat, and Matthew did a remix of Mark. Paul remixed the Gospels. Origen remixed Paul, and Tertullian remixes Origen.

You see, every generation has to do a remix. For Moses it was doo-wop. For Joshua it's hip-hop. For Moses it's a letter. For Joshua it's email. For Moses it's Aretha Franklin. For Joshua it's Alicia Keys. For Moses it's Coltrane. For Joshua it's Common. For Moses it's devotion. For Joshua it's praise and worship. For Moses it's dress up. For Joshua it's dress down. For Moses it's a hymnbook. For Joshua it's a laptop. For Moses it's a radio. For Joshua it's the Internet. For Moses it's a board. For Joshua it's a ministry. Moses is low-tech. Joshua is high-tech. Moses says, "I want to build a church." Joshua says, "I want to build a community." Moses says, "Sisters can't preach in the church." But Joshua says, "The Word says I will pour out my spirit unto all flesh!"

The only reason that Joshua could survive is that Joshua can do a remix because Moses gives him the tools to sample. Moses places his hands on Joshua! He says, "I give you what I have. You do not threaten me. I'm not going to hold you back, Joshua." But wait a minute. Joshua is not trying to push Moses aside.

He says, "We need an intergenerational ministry. I've got to respect your history, and you've got to respect my direction."

And so Moses says, "I'm putting my hands on you because I want you to be in close proximity so when God pours out on me, something might get on you." You see, Moses puts his hands upon Joshua because he wants to make sure that the authority, the wisdom, and the heritage that has been placed on him by God will pass over unto Joshua. Then, when God pours on Moses, some of what has been poured on Moses might get on Joshua.

Stop hating on your neighbor. Stop being so upset when God blesses your neighbor because when God blesses your neighbor that just means Jesus is in the neighborhood. You need to get excited about what God is doing for somebody else. Are you excited about God?

Moses puts his hands on Joshua. But when we refuse to put our hands on the next generation, then American free-market culture will eventually become the ecclesiastical norm and they will (in the words of Jeremiah Wright) think that "bling-bling means blessing." Ah, but I stopped by here to tell you that whatever you have on a material level–that ain't your blessing. Your car, your house, your job, your clothes–that ain't the blessing; that is the residue.

You see, when my grandmother was living, she used to make something called teacakes. I loved my grandmother's teacakes. When she would make them, she would allow me to stand next to her in the kitchen. She would mix up the batter, and she would pour it out into a pan. And then after she poured it out she would let me lick the residue, but she would always tell me, "Don't eat too much of the residue. You'll OD on the residue. Your real blessing is in the oven."

Some of us have overdosed on the residue. The real blessing is the power and the presence of God. You can take my house, you can take my car, you can take my clothes, but I'll still have Jesus! I'll still have joy!

But then my grandmother would do this. After the teacakes were done, she would pull them out, and I would always make the mistake of reaching my hand to the teacakes. Grandma would always slap my hands and say, "Now, these teacakes are made for you. They are your blessing, but the only way you're going to receive this blessing is to thank God for it."

And, some of us are burned by our very own blessing because we never thank God for what God has already given us. (I don't know if I have somebody here.) Can you thank God right now for what God has done for you? You need to give him praise for what God is doing and what God will continue to do.

So Moses is dead, but Joshua is alive. You see, God is doing a new thing. The Bible says that every place you set your foot will be yours. Whether you go North, whether you go South, whether you go East, or whether you go West,

God says, "As I was with Moses, I will be with you. I will never leave you nor forsake you. Because I'm doing a new thing." Bless the Lord right now for what God is going to do. God's about to do a new thing! Is there anybody here? Are you ready? Are you ready? Give God some praise! That was then, but this is now!

Notes

[1] This article first appeared in the Volume 10, Number 1, Winter 2007 issue of *The African American Pulpit* and is reprinted with the author's permission.
[2] Matthew 4:4, NIV; see also Deuteronomy 8:3.
[3] Luke 4:18; see also Isaiah 61:1.
[4] Matthew 5:43-44.

Emerging Possibilities for African American Worship

DOUG POWE

Interest in anything *emerging* continues to grow as "emerging" becomes the new buzzword in the church. Those deeply committed to emerging conversations, however, are not interested in being subsumed into another ten-step program aimed at renewing worship. Those committed to the emergent dialogue perceive a cultural shift occurring within society that cannot be ignored any longer by the church. The shift from modernity to postmodernity or from privileging self-autonomy to reclaiming holistic understandings of community is one way to describe this move. Because the emergent conversation is about a cultural shift in society it involves all of church life and not just worship.

Unfortunately as important as this emergent conversation is for the church and the culture it has typically been monophonic. I say monophonic because Euro-American voices are currently shaping the dialogue.[1] Therefore, my goal in this article is to raise three questions related to how and if African Americans should participate in the emerging dialogue: 1) What is emergent? 2) Are there emergent possibilities for those within the African American community? and 3) What does considering emergent mean for African American worship?

What Is Emergent?

Emergent is many things. One way to describe the conversation is as an attempt to break modernity's hold on the church by moving away from rationalistic and individualistic ways of understanding Christianity. Those within the emergent conversation are moving towards postmodernity, which attempts to embrace a more communal and relational understanding of Christianity. Tim Condor, a pastor in North Carolina, describes this phenomenon in the following manner:

> As a pastor who has many friendships and relationships outside of the church, I often feel like I'm standing in a dark, deep chasm between two cliffs. On one towering precipice stands the church, with its long history of effective ministry empowered by a passionate faith in Jesus that humbles and challenges me. But atop the other is a radically changed world that reflexively finds the language, idioms, assumptions, and affirmations of the church–when it considers them all–to be irrelevant, alien, impenetrable, or even oppressive.[2]

Condor describes the challenge many churches in America face today, including African American churches. The church tries to bridge the chasm between a particular way of understanding the Christian faith shaped by the past and seeking to connect this faith with individuals living with postmodern sensibilities. Individuals engaged in the emergent conversation make connections between those with late twentieth-/early twenty-first century experiences and expectations and Christian faith. They move away from "neck-up" faith, to a faith that intentionally embraces mystery and embodied worship. For example, many emergent worship services engage all of the senses through various means and not simply one or two senses.

The idea is that we bring all of ourselves to God in worship, and not just a part of who we are. Worship includes "our words (and our inner speech), our emotions, our thoughts our actions, and our relationships".[3] Trying to compartmentalize any aspect of who we are in worship means we are left to look for wholeness in other places as we seek to make meaning out of our lives. Worship does not become the ultimate answer to all of the ills of society, but it does mean worship is no longer just one more checkmark on the weekly to-do list, but a significant experience in life.

A legacy from modernity is fragmentation or the need to compartmentalize things into knowable categories. This fragmentation has tended to segment worship from the rest of life and emphasize only the cognitive aspects of worship. Postmodernity seeks to rediscover ancient forms of Christian community that retain the mystery and awe of God. Emergent conversationalists help individuals experience God by allowing openness to the mystery of God without a need to rationalize every aspect of faith. African and African Americans understand the experience of mystery as expressed in the church's relationship with the Spirit. But emergent thought moves this mystery from the individual's experience with God to the community's experience and highlights this communal nature.[4]

Are There Emergent Possibilities for the African American Church?

Many within the African American church community would not perceive ideas like greater parishioner participation and experiential worship as inconsistent with the black church. Participation by parishioners during worship is perceived as a good thing and not something to be frowned upon. In fact, many within the African American community will argue this movement is nothing new since numerous black churches have always had these characteristics. While it is certainly true that many African American churches are participatory, experiential, and relational, these churches are not emergent in the way those within the emerging conversation use the term. The difference is many African American churches are not explicitly thinking about the cultural shift from modernity to postmodernity and the implications this has for the church. For example, many African American congregations are still relying on a 1960s model of worship with some expanded options.

Because many African American churches are trapped in a 1960s model of worship they struggle to attract and keep the twenty and thirty-years-olds in church.[5] Let me be clear that doing "emerging things" will not resolve this issue, but engaging the emerging dialogue can help African Americans think through what the on-going cultural shift means for our community. Brian McLaren, one of the most prolific writers in the emerging conversation, suggests:

> If you are a Christian of any sort–liberal, conservative, evangelical, mainline, Catholic, Protestant, hand-clapper, non-clapper, devotee of pipe organ or keyboard, of piano or guitar–or even if you are not a Christian, you recognize that these grinding, shifting, transitional times have shaken the church.[6]

McLaren is right; these transitional times have shaken the church and this includes the African American church. The African American church cannot take for granted that those within the community perceive it as something other than an institution. For many within the African American community, the church no longer helps to make meaning for one's life.

The emerging conversation has something to offer individuals within the African American community who are disconnected or disappointed with the church. One possible connection between emergent folk and the African American community may be the hip-hop culture. Hip-hop is more than rap music and it is more diverse than the misogynistic lyrics espoused by some male rap artists.[7] Efrem Smith a pastor in Minneapolis argues, "hip-hip is about dance, art, expression, pain, love, racism, sexism, broken families, hard times, the search for God and overcoming."[8] His point is that limiting hip-hop to only rap music is a mistake made by many outsiders.

Because hip-hop is a product of the postmodern culture, African Americans within hip-hop are in a position to understand the cultural shift those in the emerging church are arguing for in Christianity. Rethinking African American worship from a hip-hop perspective including art, music, dance, and incense would be congruent with what is happening in emerging conversations. Many people within the hip-hop culture cannot connect to the language or idioms used by traditional protestant denominations (e.g., United Methodist Church), but this inability to connect does not mean faith is not important to them. Worship leaders are challenged to communicate a theologically sound message in a way that is authentic to those within the hip-hop culture and help them to express their faith.

African American churches face this challenge more and more as they try to get intergenerational involvement in worship. Some churches have moved to a more contemporary worship service or have added contemporary pieces to their worship service. Adding contemporary elements to a worship service is fine, but it does not make it emergent or hip-hop. Churches have to shift their mindset and perspective. Not every church is suited for such a shift and not every church should attempt such a shift. But some already have, are trying it now, or are primed for the move.

What Does Considering Emergent Mean for African American Worship?

I have been careful in this article to point out that limiting emergent ideas to worship is a mistake made by those outside of the emergent conversation. The emergent conversation is really about a cultural shift occurring within society.

Yet, I will sin boldly and give four suggestions for how the emergent conversation and African American churches can dialogue about worship.

First, the emergent conversation can influence some African American churches to rethink some of the dualisms present in our worshipping communities. By this I mean the split between faith/reason and heart/mind.[9] In some African American circles, someone with education is suspect as a pastor because that individual is not truly guided by faith or the Spirit in the minds of some. Or sometimes it is said we must believe with our hearts and not think about what the Bible tells us too much. These are over simplifications, but representative of some of the dualisms present in African American worship. Those within the emergent conversation do not buy into simplistic dualisms and believe faith/reason and heart/mind are not mutually exclusive notions. We come as whole people to God in worship and these notions of who we are as people can be held together in ways that are not dualistic. This shift requires a fearless facing of our assumptions about faith, the Bible, and the tensions within text and context.

Second, the emergent conversation can influence some African American churches to consider what qualifies as worship. Some African American churches have predetermined ideas about what worship should be and who should participate. Those within the emergent conversation focus on telling the gospel story, but the manner in which it is told can vary. The gospel does not have to be preached in a "certain way" and the choir does not have to sing in a "certain way" to qualify as worship. The openness to think about telling the story in a variety of ways could enhance some African American worship services. For example, a so-called "secular" song might be used to start a dialogue sermon.

Third, African American churches can influence the emergent conversation by expanding the dialogue to include more diverse participants. A dialogue between those in the hip-hop culture and the emergent culture could be fruitful for re-conceptualizing worship as we move deeper into postmodernity. Those in the hip-hop culture are on the cutting edge of postmodernity within the African American community and a conversation with those committed to the emergent dialogue could move churches toward a unique worship experience that often is not possible in most churches currently. The challenge will be maintaining theological credibility while communicating the gospel in a different manner.

Fourth, African American churches can influence the emergent conversation in the way that many congregations are able to interpret Christian idioms for the black community. A commitment to the teaching of the elders already positions African and African Americans to create griot-circles where the past, present, and future learn from one another in the same room. Although the emergent conversation has not focused on building bridges to the past, connections need to occur if it wants the broader Christian community to participate in the conversation. Emergent thought can learn from some African American churches how to build these bridges in a way that translates the content of their message without losing the impact of the message. Because African and African Americans often find themselves "translating" the dominant culture into the language of the margins, they are uniquely positioned to enter this discourse. They can help people see the shift as not just a "white thing," a twelve-step program, or a passing fad, but rather the move of God into the future.

There are some benefits in African American churches participating in the emerging conversation as long as we keep in mind cultural relevance. Those in the emerging conversation are trying to stay faithful to the gospel and communicate it to others in creative ways. Those of us in the African American community should seek to do the same or our worship services will seem to be empty of meaning and ritualistic for many, both inside and outside of the Christian community.

Notes

[1] The conversation is by no means exclusively European American, but European Americans are the predominate voices shaping the conversation at this point. Karen Ward the pastor of Church of the Apostles is one example of an African American fully engaged in the conversation.

[2] Tim Condor, *The Church in Transition* (Grand Rapids, MI: Zondervan, 2006), 13.

[3] Ibid., 192.

[4] Barbara A. Holmes, *Joy Unspeakable: Contemplative Practices of the Black Church* (Augsburg Fortress Press, 2004).

[5] It is unfair to claim the emerging conversation is limited only to twenty and thirty-year-olds, but it is fair to say many in this age span are shaped by postmodernity in ways that their parents are not.

[6] Brian D. McLaren, *The Church on the Other Side* (Grand Rapids, MI: Zondervan, 2000), 13.

[7] Making this claim in no way supports the lyrics of the artists who engage in demeaning women, but it is an effort to help people not frame hip-hop into a one-dimensional box.

[8] Phil Jackson and Efrem Smith, *The Hip-Hop Church* (Downers Grove, Illinois: Intervarsity Press, 2005), 61.

[9] Henry H. Knight, III, "John Wesley and The Emerging Church," published online at UMerging.org, 4.

Technologies for Worship

ELONDA CLAY

The movement to use information technologies has mushroomed in many local Africana churches. Churches already use information technologies, such as computers, mobile devices, and the Internet, for administration, worship, education, and evangelism purposes. For this reason, technologies for worship are a particular topic of concern as Africana worship enters the twenty-first century.

What are technologies for worship and what do they do? Technologies for worship include computers and software, sound systems and microphones, lighting systems, video systems (cameras, projectors, screens, and graphics software), compact discs and tape-duplicating devices, audio/visual production, and editing systems. These technologies merge multimedia computers with communications and broadcast media technologies. They should enhance the worship experience for the congregation, not set the agenda for worship itself. Technologies for worship help distribute the Christian message to wider audiences and serve as an opportunity to encourage others in the community.

More recently, multimedia preaching has been increasingly applied in local churches. This approach uses presentation software to share images or video clips directly related to the worship theme. Because many persons are visual learners, the addition of visual aids can help them remember important points. One challenge for multimedia preaching in Africana worship is the sparse availability of Africana digital images. A solution to this problem may be to use local pictures or to include images from nature and Africana culture.

Africana Christian communities often use information technologies to maintain contact with loved ones who are living long distances from one another. While traveling away from home, these persons are grateful for the opportunity to stay up-to-date on church happenings. Some congregations take advantage of technologies for worship by broadcasting worship services over the Internet or making worship services available as a podcast (multimedia file for personal audio players). Others record worship services onto compact discs (CDs), DVDs or videotapes prior to broadcasting them on local radio and television stations.

Media ministry is a specialized ministry, often requiring the assistance of persons with considerable technical skill and training. Oftentimes, there are few technical lay volunteers, which means those who can volunteer in this ministry risk endangering their personal worship and spirituality because they cannot take a break. They may experience burnout, but feel obligated to continue in their work. Churches should, whenever possible, have rotating teams that operate technologies for worship or consider hiring a media ministry person to a staff position.

In spite of all the preworship-planning and equipment-checking that go with using worship technology, unexpected malfunctions do occur. In situations such as these, a little grace towards the media ministry team goes a long way.

Technicians or church committees frequently are the ones who make recommendations to guide technology purchases. Pastors, often very busy with their duties, do need to have some sense of the big picture of technology within local churches. A lack of understanding or planning for technology may lead to overspending, the selection of obsolete technology, mishandling of technical volunteers, or sometimes the loss of important church information.

Finally, here are some general recommendations in the spirit of the Book of Discipline on technology and the local church. First, decisions about the use of technologies within churches should be rooted in practical theology and ministry. Consult the denomination's Social Principles concerning Information Communication Technology[1]; also, study the mission statement of the local church. Before any equipment is purchased or a project using new technology is taken up, we might ask these questions: Will this equipment enhance the nurture, witness, and outreach of our congregation? How do we measure the results?

Second, wisdom must play a vital role in how we use technologies for worship. Insure that practices do not exclude persons within the congregation.

Remember that an inequality of access to information technologies exists in our congregations and our communities. We must make sure that by saying, "It's on the church's website," we take this inequality into account.

Third, remember that youth and young adults are usually more enthusiastic about the use of technology than some middle-aged adult leaders. Empowering youth and young adults to operate technologies for worship provides them with an opportunity to both serve the church and to learn skills that will help them in the future. The church provides them with a holistic environment that can emphasize responsibility and critical engagement with these technologies, making a meaningful contribution to both the local and global Africana communities.

Notes

[1] *The Social Principles of the United Methodist Church*, "Information Communication Technology" http://archives.umc.org/interior.asp?ptid=1&mid=1763

"Lord, How Come We Here?"[1]

WILLIAM B. MCCLAIN

For insight on the meaning of worship and spirituality from an Africana perspective, we pose the question, **"Lord, how come we here?"** It is a simple question in the idiom of the people who first raised it that way. I believe this question can be spoken again in this way–even in the twenty-first century–for two reasons: (1) because God speaks to our human experience and not to our affectations, and (2) because the profound expressions of African people, and in particular, African American people who raised it in this profound, grammatical way, were shaped in a terrible time of uprootedness and transition.

They raised this question as the Africans' first encounter with God in America came, when they were struggling to bridge the communication gap and the cultural gap between themselves and their captors. The language patterns they developed were a hybrid of their native language(s) and that of the host society. Just as the host language was imperfectly understood, so was the Africans' sense of being and purpose confused by their arrival in a new and alien land.

How come we here? was a very logical question for the Africans to raise in this new setting: forcibly torn from their homeland and the routine of their settled lives in their own villages and towns without their consent; herded on death ships like cattle to come to America to be slaves to their capriciously cruel captors; auctioned off in the marketplace–not even as human beings–but mere property to be bought, owned and used; stripped of every vestige of their dignity and respectability; kin separated from kin, tribe separated from tribe, sons and daughters separated from mothers and fathers, and all separated from the place of spiritual and human meaning in their lives. In this strange land to which they were brought to bear these unusual and heavy burdens, the spiritual strivings and wrestlings began; i.e., the soul's inquiry into the worth, meaning, and purpose of their lives. **"Lord, how come we here?"** is asked in an effort to bridge the communication gap. The spiritual implications of the question are vast indeed.

The spiritual strivings of these transplanted Africans began long before, and continued long after, the so-called "Magnolia Missions" of white Christians converted them to Christianity and had a chance to plant the heretical notion that these Africans had no identity and were cursed and ordained by God to be but "hewers of wood" and "drawers of water." Even though they were stripped of everything of their former lives and left with nothing else of their prior selves but a mere gossamer of their spiritual identity, these involuntarily depersonalized expatriate souls used this last fragile fiber of faith–half-forgotten and therefore half-remembered–to ponder the most piercingly profound and perennial of spiritual questions: **"Lord, how come we here?"**

The spiritual implications of the question would take on ever-increasing significance as the developing African American experience unfolded in the complex, diverse, and human relationships that make that experience unique. Clearly, the question: **how come we here?** is much easier to explain than it is to answer. That requires the complete acceptance of God's inscrutable agenda, by faith alone. The obvious answer is that we are here because God has chosen to bring us here. But it is the "why" behind the divine choice that we truly long to understand. We know by faith that in the Divine Scheme "all things work together for good," but what we do not know, and cannot know, is, "all things." We see through a glass darkly and perhaps dimly, and that is because we are mortal and our vision is limited. We will see more clearly when a level of faith we have not yet achieved improves our vision.

In the meantime, life has to be lived and confronted on a daily basis, for survival itself is the first condition of "survival-for-what?" If we are not here when the glass is cleared and the revelation is made, then we will never know **"how come we here?"**

In their struggle with the "in the meantime," African Americans have made an effort to deal with this spiritual question and to appropriate the meaning of suffering and their experience of pain with expressions of soulful soliloquies, songs, sayings, sermons, and shouts; but also dances, confessions, poems, raps, and other forms of spiritual responses. All are a part of the "stuff" that forms and informs African American spirituality. All are a part of what my late teacher Howard Thurman at Boston University used to call their "life's working paper." For, in a real sense, it is made up of the creative combination of what a people are in their many and various parts and how they react to the process of living. There are the personal and deep longings of every African American (even among those who act it out in rage and strange and utterly destructive behavior) to be simply viewed and received just like everybody else, as who they are, and to be free to be themselves on their own terms: just "one of God's children" with strengths and weaknesses, gifts and limitations, and all of the rest of the characteristics common to the human lot. And, yet again, African Americans are tied to others who share a common heritage, history, and hope, and who look like themselves–sing and shout, pray and die–even though sometimes in a different mien.

In its many facets and in so many different ways, African American spirituality as expressed in worship identifies its suffering with Moses and the Hebrew children, and their struggle and suffering, and the Hebrews who insisted that any Pharaoh who holds the children in bondage must let God's people go by whatever means the Lord chooses! For as so many faithful African Americans put it, "You are God *all by yourself!*" This means that even if God has to roll back the waters of the Red Sea and drown Pharaoh's army, or cause "Jordan to stand still," God's children have to get to the Promised Land of freedom. At the heart of any form of African American spirituality that is true to its Africana roots and a Wesleyan heritage is the unquestionable, uncontestable, undebateable, orthodox, and dogmatic belief that the act of the liberating of God's people is an amazing act of divine grace.

It would be unfair and untrue to simply paint the picture of Africana worship and African American spirituality, or the worship and spirituality of any people, as only a life of struggle and merely a response to suffering. There is always within its very fiber a fierce and abiding sense of justice and what is right, and a response to the active presence of **grace**, and even **"grace upon grace,"** (especially among Wesleyans and Methodists of whatever stripe),[2] as they ponder the question, **"Lord, how come we here?"** In doing so, they incorporate into their struggle for meaning the notions of justice, freedom, and love.

African American spirituality is also a response to God's act of grace. We hear it in the classical and traditional prayer of the old-fashioned steward (an office still maintained in the black denominational Methodist churches, and even in some African American United Methodist Churches. When I served as pastor of Union United Methodist Church in Boston for ten years, that church continued the tradition of the office of steward, even when the national church had abandoned it.) As I tried to point out in an earlier work I wrote, *Come Sunday: The Liturgy of Zion*, it does not matter at all that this same prayer was prayed last Sunday or Wednesday night at prayer meeting or at any number of other worship settings. It is still the African American response to grace and one of the answers to the spiritual question: **"Lord, how come we here?"**

In the words of one of the stewards or one of the other prayer warriors as they come before the throne of grace, knee-bowed and body bent:

> "We thank you that you watched over us all night long while we slumbered and slept in the very image of death. Early this morning you touched us with the fingertip of love . . . I want to thank you that when I rose this morning, my bed was not my cooling board and my sheet was not my winding cloth. Through your goodness and mercy you have seen fit to leave us here to pick and choose our own praying ground. We thank you for protecting us from dangers, seen and unseen. We thank you for leading us from one good degree of grace to another . . . "[3]

Human survival seems to be threatened by the hour. The struggle to be witnesses and to participate in God's plan for the coming of the Kingdom cannot be separated from the struggle to survive our cultural holocaust. Spirituality as expressed in worship is the glue that connects the two struggles. In an age of rage, it is a counsel of reconciliation; in an age of hostility, it promotes healing; as we struggle with evil and imperfection, it encourages us to appreciate and glorify what is positive and good. It reminds us that there is good in all of us because there is God in each of us. When the world beats us down, dismisses us as worthless, calls us everything else but a child of God, Africana spirituality reminds us that we are a chosen people, chosen for a task not yet fully revealed, but we can wait on the Lord, patiently and faithfully, until our time comes. It reminds us that we must be ready when God is ready. That's why we are here and why we can celebrate God's gracious gifts to us, and that is why we are rejoicing that we are here.

We hear the African American response to the experience of grace as the people gather, whether there be two or three, or two or three thousands, singing and praising God and shouting about "Your grace and mercy brought me through, living each moment all because of you. I want to thank you and praise you, too. Your grace and mercy brought me through." Some quietly, with reverence in their hearts and thanksgiving within the very depths of their grateful souls, give thanks for this miraculous pouring out of this matchless, unfathomable, unspeakable and amazing grace. Others may even quietly wipe away the tears of joy. It is their own response to the question, **"Lord, how come we here?"** But some of the people cannot be quiet, nor can they be still. They can contain themselves no longer. To avoid the "rocks crying out" in response to the presence, reality, and manifestation of God's overwhelming grace, they shout and scream out as if their whole selves–mind, soul, spirit, and body–have been taken over, possessed by an unseen controlling force beyond the ability of any human eyes to perceive. Their responses are passionate, and their emotional outpourings are often tears of joy, praise, and thanksgiving, sometimes unintelligible as if it came from another world, and some even dance between the pews and in the aisles. Their uncontrollable screams, shouts and chants begin decipherably and crystal clear: "Hallelujah! Thank you, Jesus! Praise the Lord! Hallelujah!" Not everyone, but some said, "Lord, that is how come we are here!"

So, in a real sense, and in a Wesleyan perspective with Africana roots and Methodist identity, African American spirituality is a response to the reality of suffering, as well as a response to the experience of grace. The effort in *The Africana Worship Book* series on the part of the writers is another way of helping us respond to suffering and grace in a Wesleyan key. The faithful and able authors of these worship helps in poems and prayers, litanies and meditations, invitations to discipleship, creedal statements, and many other useful worship aids have tried to help us continue to respond to the question: **"Lord, how come we here?"**

Several of them are former students of mine, some in the Wesley Theological Seminary regular Master's programs, others in doctoral programs, and still others in programs or settings where I have had the privilege and honor, by God's grace, to be their teacher and mentor. I commend them for work well done, and I commend and recommend their offerings as wonderful gifts to help the *whole* church respond to the experience of God's grace. Indeed, that is what true worship is: to remember where we have known God's grace, even in the midst of persecution, suffering, trials, and all manner of injustice, to be challenged to face the present with faith and courage, and to have hope about the future. That is what true worship is: for the people of God to gather around the Word and the sacrament and to stand in the present with one hand grasping the past and the other reaching toward the future.

The truth is, the question from Africana **"Lord, how come we here?"** is really a question for all worshipers to raise in whatever denomination, or whatever region of the world, or whatever culture, or whatever ethnic group, as they come into God's sanctuary. Or, in the words of the General Editor of

The Africana Worship Book series, Dr. Valerie Bridgeman Davis: as hearts are "open to the flame of God's presence in the Spirit," we might ask afresh the question, and with all of our twenty-first century sophistication in communications and technology, **"Lord, how come we here?"**

Notes

[1] This article first appeared as the foreword to *The Africana Worship Book, Year A (Nashville: Discipleship Resources, 2006)*, and is reprinted with the author's permission.
[2] See William B. McClain, *Black People in The Methodist Church: Whither Thou Goest* (Nashville: Abingdon Press, 1984), for a discussion of Wesleyan groups, the theology, and their common history and heritage, especially pp. 15ff. See also Grant S. Shockley, Heritage and Hope: The African American Presence in United Methodism (Nashville: Abingdon Press, 1991).
[3] Excerpt from *Come Sunday: The Liturgy of Zion* by William McClain © 1990 by Abingdon Press Used by permission. See also Frederick Hilborn Talbot, *African American Worship: New Eyes for Seeing* (Lima, Ohio: Fairway Press, 1998, pp. 72-73 for a version of this prayer heard in the AME. Church. There are many variations on this classical African American prayer with denominational, regional, and doctrinal nuances and emphases, e.g., whether it is a Deacon in Baptist circles or stewards and others in Wesleyan and various African American churches.

Spiritual Focus and Africana Worship

HENRY H. MITCHELL

One Sunday, my wife Ella and I preached a dialogue sermon from 2 Timothy 4. The text was assigned; we had led a Bible study from the chapter the day before, and we were trying to keep focus in one place for the weekend. Our preaching text was verse 7a: "I am now ready to be offered . . ." The sermon was titled, "Getting Ready," and the invitational hymn was the spiritual, "I Want To Be Ready." We had not given the church notice of our theme. But before the sermon, the choir sang an anthem that included the same theme of "getting ready."

Of course, we need not have been so surprised. This sort of spiritual focus happens all too often for us to think of it as anything less than providential planning, or divine guidance. At the time of planning, a worship leader may or may not be aware of just how much help God has given. It all comes out in hindsight. In our case, we had certainly not expected such affirmation and confirmation of our labor, so we were deeply moved looking back in wonder and joy. We had in fact done our best praying and preparing, but it had happened too late for us to inform the host church of our theme focus. It had to be God who guided them.

The insight to be gained here has to be that God the Holy Spirit wills that we carefully focus our human preparation for worship, so that the worship we plan helps us grow or improve in just one phase of Christian life. The prophet Isaiah had a metaphor for this focused preparation: "Make straight in the desert a highway for our God" (40:4, NKJV). In the experience reported above, the blessing bestowed on all concerned made it plain that focus, or the concentration of our spiritual attention, is of serious concern for the worship of our God. This discipline is not "Whatever you like," even in the marvelous spontaneity of black or Africana preaching and worship. God requires that we invite God's focusing guidance during preparation for worship and for preaching, as well as during leadership of worship and delivery of sermons. Exceptions to discipline come only during dire emergencies, when the time of preparation has been crowded out. At such times the sermons God gives may be more powerful than any other. It's just that we can't make excuses and call excuses emergencies.

The greatest sins and shortcomings of the African American worship and preaching traditions occur at this point of spiritual focus. If a "team" is leading preparatory worship, and the Spirit seems not to have come yet, we do not wait for her to come; we stir her up almost by brute vocal stimulation. If we have preached our best, and the response is not enough to please the preacher, we insert stock phrases and stories "known to kill" the audience. We resort to such tactics at the risk of losing the impact of the word, spoken and sung. Consciously or no, it is a grave error to cease to relate to the text in order to stir and please the crowd.

It takes more effort to keep focused, but it is worth all the effort and more. God's providential assistance adds more when we try harder. The experience reported here ended in a host of people rejoicing, and that rejoicing was focused on a fruitful, relevant purpose of spiritual growth and Godly behavior. We dare not seek for more, nor ask God for less.

Worship: The Realm of the Spirit, the Realm of the Imagination, and Real Time[1]

MARILYN E. THORNTON

Then I looked up, and I heard the voice of many angels surrounding the throne and the living creatures and the elders; they numbered myriads of myriads and thousands of thousands, singing with full voice,

"Worthy is the Lamb that was slaughtered
to receive power and wealth and wisdom and might
and honor and glory and blessing!"

Then I heard every creature in heaven and on earth and under the earth and in the sea, and all that is in them singing,

"To the one seated upon the throne and to the Lamb
be blessing and honor and glory and might

forever and ever."
And the four creatures said "Amen!" And the elders fell down and worshipped.

Revelation 5:11-14 (NRSV)

The Revelation of John is a book that has boggled the minds and hearts of many a believer. In its pages the Apostle John, banished to the Isle of Patmos, records his experience of receiving visions so real that he not only sees them but he hears them. Its graphic imagery and hidden meanings are sources of hope for some and fear for others. The Revelation to John contains messages to churches, edicts of judgment and condemnation, descriptive accounts of wars and struggle, and of beasts and creatures, and many incidents of praise and worship.

John starts out the book in worship. Just prior to actually describing his first vision, John couches his storytelling by saying, "I was in the spirit on the Lord's day." How do we truly worship if we are not "in the spirit"? From John we know that worship occurs in the realm of the spirit, the realm of the imagination, as well as in real time. In real time John experienced persecution but in the realm of the spirit an isolated John found community; in the realm of the imagination John found answers and promise.

In our postmodern lives of sound-bytes, thirty-second commercials, and two-second conversations, when is there time or possibility to walk in the realm of the spirit? John was on an enforced retreat on the Isle of Patmos. **He** had plenty of time to meditate. The temple at Jerusalem had been destroyed and Rome was persecuting Jews and anyone connected with Jews (like Christians). John was involuntarily isolated for spreading the gospel message in the Roman world. We, however, must voluntarily create an island, a place of refuge where we can be alone with God and where our spirits can experience wholeness and love despite the terrors of living in the real world. This need to create an island is why we have stopped the clock, set time apart, and come together to create writings that will facilitate worship in our churches. We have done this so that we will have time to meditate, to engage our spirits in the creative process, and to commune with one another.

It is difficult to find time to participate in the creative process in our daily lives. Sometimes I cannot write a sermon or compose music until I am asleep. In sleep, when I have released the strictures of real time, my spirit becomes free to hear God and experience what God wants to reveal to me. I have awakened from sleep to see a gleaming moon and write a poem about it. God has awakened me with new music that will not let me go until I flesh it out on the piano in real sound. Perhaps it is at night when real time feels unmeasured that my spirit seeks a God who has sought me first. Perhaps it is at night during sleep when real situations and problems are banished to the unconscious that God is able to get a message through.

Oftentimes, we experience true worship only in the midst of crisis. At our lowest, emptiest moment we begin to understand God as one who is full and whole, that only such a God can meet us in our direst need. John was in exile, emptied of companions when he worshipped God and saw glorious visions. In August of 1998 my family was on the verge of an emotional, financial, career catastrophe. Early one morning as we all lay sleeping, resting up for the trials to come, I experienced an auditory and visual presence of God. As I lay in my bed I heard the piano playing in the living room. I saw an angel at the piano. When I awoke I wrote this poem.

This Morning (1998)

An angel played on my piano this morning,
A simple melody
That soothed the tremors of my mind
That tapped so lightly on my ear
Awakening my spirit to the early symphony.

This morning I heard an angel caressing
So lightly on the keys
A tender song I tried to grasp
As I emerged from fitful sleep
Feeling, hearing the rhythms of the insects, birds, and trees.

And as the angel was playing I could feel
God playing on my heart,
Stroking the chords of my delight,
Flooding my soul with songs of praise
Grateful for a world of wonder, new day about to start.

In the dimness of the dawn I could see her
Sitting in the shadows.
The bright day sneaking in the room,
The music blessing soul and mind;
Urging the limbs of my body to rise, and I arose.

You may not believe what I heard and saw as dawn came
With night adjourning.
It may have been imagination

Or expression of repression, but
I believe an angel played on my piano this morning.

In the midst of strife, God sought me out in my spirit so that I could receive the benefit true worship brings: the knowledge that God is always present, no matter the external circumstance. John says that he was in the spirit. As he was in the spirit, God led him into the realm of the imagination. **John** was daydreaming.

Children get in trouble for daydreaming. You've been there. Something captures the imagination and you basically lose consciousness. We tell children to come back to the real world not realizing that daydreaming is developing the mind. It is through imagination that creativity is stirred, producing real artistry, real solutions to problems, real new discoveries. Columbus dreamed of a round world when everyone else believed that it was flat. His imagination took him on a journey that discovered a real New World for Europeans. It was an Old World for the Adirondacks, the Blackfoot, the Cherokee, and just so many others but it was new to Columbus and his crew. I hope that you will spend some of the time here, daydreaming, exploring the unconscious recesses of the wonderful mind that God has given you, allowing the Holy Spirit to bring forth a creativity that you did not know that you had, producing resources that will continue to facilitate imaginative worship in our churches.

Now, there is a difference between the imaginative and the imaginary. That which is imaginary is something that is not real, was not ever real, and never will be real. It is an image that may either communicate truth through something that is obviously not real or that appears or sounds real but communicates lies. Road Runner and Bugs Bunny are obviously not real. These cartoon characters, however, go through situations that communicate truth, that the weak often overcome the strong, that those with guns and bombs, like Coyote and Elmer Fudd, are not necessarily the smarter ones. These are great truths communicated through the imaginary. The other side of being imaginary is that which appears real like voices and hallucinations in the mind of mentally deranged persons, who may believe the lie that death is better than life and move to kill themselves or another because of the very real sounding imaginary voices in their heads.

That which is spiritually imaginative can be described by the phrase "living in the imagination of God," what Paul tells us: "No eye has seen, nor ear heard, nor the human heart conceived, what God had prepared for those who love him" (1 Corinthians 2:9). Our everlasting God has an infinite imagination. At the same time, there is nothing more real than God. As we delve into the spirit, God helps us to see and to hear, helps our hearts to ascertain the images and imagery that will edify a community whose collective mind and soul are still wounded by the experience of slavery, the reality of post-affirmative action **as well as** by the pornographic and violent imprints of our twenty-first century world.

Through our daydreaming we will come up with the words that can help people move from the immobilizing circumstances of their real lives to imagining and accessing the possibilities of what God truly desires for them. By using our imaginations we will provide balm and healing for real problems that occur historically and contemporaneously in our communities. We do this not by pretending, but by acknowledging the reality of what happens in the lives of black people living in this world, the fact of Darfur, HIV/AIDS, violence and drugs in our communities, and the reality of Katrina and its continuing aftermath. We do this by acknowledging the reality of God who was able to lead us over the waters of the Middle Passage, and through the waters of the Ohio River in escaping to freedom, and up the waters of the Mississippi during the Great Migration. This same God will lead us beyond the waters of Katrina to a more holistic, life-affirming place.

With these selections that God will work out in us by the power and movement of the Holy Spirit, we may express for others that which they have been unable to express, and by naming the un-nameable of their life experience, they become freed to move forward in their lives and in their faith. Our work and our worship should be in the realm of the imagination because God is there. At the same time, our work and our worship should be an authentication and validation of our real selves, the self that God created, our black, Africana selves, whose story is part of the story of God's deliverance for all people.

John saw a congregation of angels, elders, and all living things in the universe participating in a worship service. As he sat on that island, all by himself, he found in his imagination, a community with the same purpose as he, of worshipping Almighty God. Even as John felt the pangs of persecution, the arrows of aloneness, and the daggers of dislocation, he was able to experience "a foretaste of glory divine." By the same token our worship in real time, in the real world should be an approximation of what our imaginations can conceive of "when we all get to heaven." Our work and our worship should lead our communities to hope: hope in God and hope in self, knowing that our adoration of the Lamb, Jesus Christ who sits on the throne is in communion with the saints who will be of every tribe and language and people and nation, indeed every creature in the universe!

In worship, we take real time to honor God who honored us with the sacrifice of Jesus the Lamb. Through worship, we receive the power of God to wrestle with real problems and situations. We come to realize that God is able to wipe every tear; God will strengthen us for the trials to come. In imaginative, spiritual worship we take real time to bless God and give God the glory.

Worthy is the lamb that was slain! Let us fall down and worship God! Let us live in the imagination of God! Amen!

Notes

[1] This sermon was preached on November 3, 2006 as part of the Upper Room Chapel Service at the General Board of Discipleship for the last writing workshop of the Africana Liturgy Project.

Inclusive Language and Africana Worship

VALERIE BRIDGEMAN DAVIS

> Challenges to our comfort encourage us to at least try thinking of God in ways that we often neglect in scriptural texts of our traditions, whether we are comfortable or not. –Karen Baker Fletcher

> Indeed it is not a "white thing" but a justice issue. –Dr. Jamie Phelps

"Everything we say about God is a lie."

I start almost every discussion on inclusive language in every class, no matter the topic, with this statement. In each class there are always recalcitrant and resistant students to the notion of gender-inclusive language for humans, and vehement disdain and anger when I say that "father" language is insufficient for God language. But I do not use these words for shock value. I know that to say "God is father" does not mean the man who creeps into the bedroom of his daughters (or sons) and rapes them. To say "God is mother" does not mean the woman who drowns her children in a psychotic break during postpartum depression. If we say "God is rock" we do not mean that substance that though "solid" erodes with time, wind, and rain. Therefore, the realm of God-talk is not semantics. The truth is as Sallie McFague notes, God "is she and he and neither."[1] Conversation about language is significant because language creates worlds. Or, as Brian Wren notes, "no image is adequate. To select one image and bow down to it is idolatrous. . . . Allowing God-images to *clash* is important, because it reminds us that we are approaching that which is beyond all images."[2] As a poet, I know this truth, for words are what we use to help people envision new realities.

What is at stake in this issue as it relates to worship and Africana worship in particular? If the Catholic maxim is true–"as we worship, so we live [believe]" or "how we worship reflects what we believe and determines how we will live. The law of prayer or worship is the law of life" (*lex orandi, lex credendi*)[3]–and I think it is, then how we speak of each other and of the One who gave birth to mountains and ice (Psalm 90:2, Job 38:39), matters. Theologian Elizabeth Johnson highlights the urgent importance of attending to one's language in the church. She notes:

> The way a faith community speaks about God indicates what it considers the highest good, the profoundest truth, the most appealing beauty. This language, in turn, molds the community's corporate identity and behavior as well as the individual self-understanding of its members . . . . The symbol of God functions. It is neither abstract in content nor neutral in effect, but expresses a community's bedrock convictions.[4]

Old Testament scholar Renita Weems maintains that Africana women preachers (and all women preachers in general) are in a unique and prophetic role to challenge the way in which language speaks of the divine, and of humans: "If we don't say Mother God, who will? If we don't challenge the language, who's going to challenge it?"[5]

The most recent struggles concerning God's name is long-standing, since feminists and Womanists begin to challenge the way language shapes the theology and life of the church in the 1960s and 1970s.[6] Some questioned why the black church did not embrace the cause. In her article, "'Mother to the Motherless, Father to the Fatherless': Power, Gender, and Community in an Afrocentric Biblical Tradition", sociology of religion professor Cheryl Townsend Gilkes argues that in the lexicon of black church, "everybody knows" God is not merely father, but also a mother to the motherless, an expansion of Psalm 68:5. Townsend Gilkes argues that "the mother images of God have found their way into the traditions of Africans and Afro-Americans"[7] in the way this phrase alone found parlance in songs and preaching. While I agree with her that this phrase is pervasive, I would argue that most people in Africana worship settings still hold on to an exclusively male God. Hearing the phrase "mother to the motherless" does not mean Africana communities concretely imagine God in feminine thought patterns.

I believe the most significant issue, persuasively demonstrated in several writings, is simply idolatry, choosing our thinking and beliefs over who God really is. To box God into one metaphor (or one range of metaphors) and to insist that God cannot and ought not to be seen in any other way is to deny the radical freedom of God who may be whoever God wants to be and reveal Godself however God would. We must take seriously that the Bible does not limit language about the deity to male metaphors even if the most pervasive ones are male-centered. God's name, revealed to Moses, is an unpronounceable and untranslatable word, though it essentially means something like "God is." There is an *isness* to God that cannot be contained in any one metaphor. Though the biblical imagery of the deity is overwhelmingly male, male images are not the only images found in the Bible. For example, Psalm 22:9–10 speaks of God as the midwife, Isaiah 49:15 as a nursing mother, Hosea 13:8 as a she-bear robbed of her cubs; a mother eagle who bears her fledglings on her wings (Deuteronomy 32:11–12), a mother who comforts her child on her knee (Isaiah 66:13), an infection, a festering sore (Hosea 5:12–14), a mother hen who gathers chicks, and a woman searching for a lost coin (Luke 15:8–10) to name a few.[8]

Wren demonstrates we must name God truthfully or we will worship an idol. Language matters, he says, because "it is a fair assumption that persistent and systematic uses of language express what the speakers really think and match how they behave. Equally, it is a fair assumption that the way we speak of God shapes and slants our understanding."[9] In other words, when we refuse to consider other models, we act out of our stubborn idolatry.

Speech matters because when we hold on to oppressive models we reject more egalitarian and inclusive ones. (God as friend and lover in a mutual relationship is hard for many Africana people to imagine since many Africana cultures are macho and misogynistic in the way male-female relationships are "just understood"). I contend that the way we talk about God affects the way we relate to one another. This language conundrum includes human relationship with the rest of creation as well. For a people who believe that the earth is given as a gift that needs care, dominion language often allows us to abuse the gift, thereby despising the Giver. Arguing to expand our metaphors of the Holy beyond militaristic, conquering language, McFague made this point when she noted that "if our situation is one in which we know that we have the power to destroy ourselves and other forms of life, then power understood as domination and control, as absolute mastery and sovereignty, is counterproductive."[10]

I believe part of the reason this question is so difficult in Africana circles is that African and African descent worshiping community–and this is a gross generalization–often are Jesus-only in their worship, even when professing to be Trinitarian in beliefs. In other words, black folk love Jesus. And since Jesus is God, then God is "he."[11] There is very little distinction between the Jesus of human history and the God of eternity. In addition, the Trinitarian formula of the historic church–Father, Son, and Holy Ghost–found its way into the lore, song, and language of Africana worshipers. Many learned to read from the King James translation of the Bible; plus the poetic cadence of the archaic English still holds sway for many people.

What may pastors and worship leaders do to move the church in the direction of inclusive language? The first thing I would say is "convert." Pastors, songwriters, and worship leaders often are the front line of change in any worship setting. Start by studying scriptures with an eye toward its own diversity of God-language. Now there are many books and articles to read and ponder that will help with this process. Commit to learn why this question of inclusive language is more than *political correctness*, as critics dismiss it; it is a theological importance of our times that moves us beyond the concrete in which we have encased God to a discipline of discovery.

Secondly, I would say *be pastoral.* People do not change easily, but given good teaching and time, people may be led to a deeper relationship with God. Introduce change in language slowly. For example, start with human language. There is no good reason to continue to insist that "man" means men and women. When I turned the tables on students in a lecture and used only feminine pronouns, several students–women and men–talked with me about their discomfort that I had "excluded" men from the conversation. I explained that when I said "woman" I was including everybody, that I was using the word generically, and that "woman" meant men and women. When they argued with me, I pointed out that we have been using "man" generically for centuries. It was a teachable moment. After this experience, they each, to a person, began to use inclusive human language. Similarly, I make this same point by asking someone I know who has sisters and brothers to name her brothers. She will never name her sisters. When I argue with her that she should have named her sisters since "brothers" include all of us, she often argues me down. Again, I have succeeded in making the point that these words are not as "generic" as we like to claim. These changes can be instituted in worship by thoughtful and deliberate preparation. Even songs may be changed to reflect this inclusion.

I think, also, that God-language can be challenged in a pastoral manner.

Slow inclusion of non-gendered language like "Lover God," "Friend of Friends," and "God of Mountains and Wind," for example may be applied beyond male and female language. However, gender-specific language can be used in a pastoral way. Of course, there is the option of non-gendered language for the Holy, but since we think in binary terms, I believe a corrective in the church could begin with the good use of feminine language. For example, I was asked to bless a child in our church one Sunday. In my blessing I asked that God who comforts us on her knees like a mother and throws us in the air like a father ground this child in safety and adventure. Afterwards, several people approached me, many with tears in their eyes, and thanked me for the blessing. I had used inclusive God-language in the liturgical setting without making a big deal of it. And it had blessed the congregation.

Thirdly, experiment with different translations of the Bible. I consider the KJV a poor translation, translated from a translation and I refuse to continue to perpetrate bibliolatry by blind devotion to it. But every translation has its challenges, since all translation is interpretation. A good student of the Bible must be willing to weigh the choices and make an ethical decision with which she or he can live.

These examples and illustrations are only a start toward the work I believe we must do in Africana churches to shatter patriarchal language use that continues to hold us in unhealthy relationships with one another and with God. The struggle around how to speak of God is long-standing and not likely to end any time soon. Notwithstanding, it is a conversation that must continue if we want our worship and our lives to reflect the God of Harriet Tubman who led a many a slave out of bondage.

Notes

[1] Sallie McFague, *Models of God: Theology for an Ecological, Nuclear Age* (Philadelphia: Fortress Press, 1987), 99.

[2] Brian Wren, *What Language Shall I Borrow? God-Talk in Worship: A Male Response to Feminist Theology* (New York: The Crossroad Publishing Co., 1991), 132.

[3] Keith Fournier, "Lex Orandi, Lex Credendi: As We Worship, So We Will Live," Catholic Online. http://www.catholic.org/featured/headline.php?ID=2367. Accessed August 31, 2007.

[4] Elizabeth A. Johnson, "A Theological Case for God-She: Expanding the Treasury of Metaphor," *Commonweal*, January 29, 1993, 11–12.

[5] Renita Weems, "How Will our Preaching be Remembered? A Challenge to See the Bible form a Woman's Perspective," in *The African American Pulpit* (Summer 2006): 26–29, p. 28.

[6] I want to acknowledge that many mystics and contemplatives throughout church history

have experienced God in feminine form long before the "second wave" of feminism of the 1960s onward.

[7] Cheryl Townsend Gilkes, "Mother to the Motherless, Father to the Fatherless": Power, Gender, and Community in an Afrocentric Biblical Tradition," in *Semeia* no. 47 (1989): 57–85, p. 73.

[8] For a persuasive argument of God as a mid-wife, see Christie Cozad Neuger, "Image and Imagination: Why Inclusive Language Matters," 153–165, in *Engaging the Bible in a Gendered World: An Introduction to Feminist Biblical Interpretation in Honor of Katharine Doob Sakenfeld*, Linda Day and Carolyn Pressler, eds. (Louisville: Westminster John Knox Press, 2006). Two other good resources concerning feminine imagery for God include Virginia Ramsey Mollenkott, *The Divine Feminine: The Bible Imagery of God as Female* (New York: Crossroad, 1983) and Elizabeth A. Johnson, *She Who Is: The Mystery of God is Feminist Theological Discourse* (New York: Crossroad Publishing, 1992).

[9] Wren, 61, 70.

[10] McFague, 16.

[11] No one makes this case better than Jacquelyn Grant in her book, *White Women's Christ and Black Women's Jesus: Feminist Christology and Womanist Response* (American Academy of Religion Academy Series, No. 64) Atlanta: Scholar's Press, 1989.

Testify!

WILMA L. TAYLOR

Personal testimony is an important and intricate part of the Afrocentric worship experience. Often, these testimonies describe the process as well as the outcome of our confidence in the fact that God will see us through difficulties we encounter. Issues related to health are often the subject of our testimonies, and we strengthen one another by the witness we share. It is my hope that this testimony will offer hope to anyone struggling with difficulties related to being in good health.

In January of 2006, I had my third major abdominal surgery. Prior to this surgery, the doctor explained the possibility I might have cancer. While I was concerned with the outcome, the decision to wait and hear definitive news was the only course of action. So, I waited.

Recuperation went smoothly as I rested and took time for self-care. My days were spent relaxing from the stresses of work, and I enjoyed both the calm and the opportunity to engage in different thoughts and activities. I began to enjoy music again, took time to meditate, and read the Bible in the quiet of midday. Gospel music refreshed my soul and brought memories of singing in choirs, listening to sermons, preaching sermons, and the warm embrace of people and I longed to be in worship service again.

My family and I decided several months earlier to move to another state. Now, in addition to recuperation, efforts to organize, pack, and say good-bye to a community we had known for almost thirteen years became the focus of my attention. I enjoyed office, private, and community parties with their expressions of love. I promised to return and visit. I shared telephone numbers and addresses. I met for meaningful lunches at Bob Evans Restaurant. I loved the sisterhood being demonstrated and it reminded me of community presence. I longed to be part of a worshipping community.

On January 17, the doctor told me I had cancer. I felt heart pain and earache when I heard those words. The doctor put her hand on my shoulder and explained the next steps, which included another surgery. This surgery would be referred to an oncologist who understood the details of the particular cancer I had. When I left the doctor's office, I returned home and sat in my car listening to gospel music. I needed to feel the presence of something familiar, something that would offer me comfort from the distress of recent memory and present conditions. Once again, I longed to be part of a worshipping community.

When we reached our new home, I sought a place to worship. I needed the experience of being in church on Sunday again. I needed to see the people dressed as if they had a special engagement to attend. I needed to touch freshly printed bulletins. I needed to see the ushers. I needed to sit in the pew. I needed to hear the choir sing and the worship service begin. I needed to hear the Morning Prayer, announcements, and be a part of welcoming visitors. I need to hear a sermon. I longed to be in the worship service.

In June, we decided my cancer surgery would be performed in another state. I had to travel for many tests and evaluations. The following month, my family and I journeyed to have this work completed. The oncologist surgeon said it would be a lengthy surgery and he wanted to delay it a few more weeks, especially since I had surgery the earlier part of the year. We returned home.

At church one Sunday, I heard about a sister church in an adjacent city. We visited and the connection was immediate for us. The people were warm and welcomed us. I enjoyed listening to the choir, watching the ushers, hearing the sermon, sitting in the pulpit and participating in the worship service. I had begun to feel well. I felt stronger each week I went. I felt renewed hope as a member of my new family.

On September 19, the surgery was performed. This time, my stay in the hospital was more trying. I was not able to eat for two days and when I did, it was taxing. I developed pneumonia and had high dosages of antibiotics, which caused fever blisters on my lips. The pain medication made my legs itch severely. I was given insulin for the first time in my life and my body was retaining fluid.

I thank God for my husband, who scratched my legs, bathed me, and helped me walk in the wee hours of the morning. My mother and sister traveled a great distance to be with local family members and me; all brought the Church with them. And, I longed to participate in the worship service again.

We returned home and I had a lengthy recuperation period. I was not able to sit up for more than a half hour and had trouble moving unassisted. Nonetheless, I was glad to be home and have life. It was a blessing to play with my granddaughter and laugh with my daughter. I talked with other family members and girlfriends from junior high school and felt the joy of living.

When I returned to church, the pastor preached about the death of Lazarus and the responses of his sisters, Mary and Martha. The sermon was entitled, "A Case for a Miracle." I was fascinated and began to put my own context in the sermon. I felt that Jesus had called me from dark places of death to the light of life. It was Jesus who did the calling, and the community was the witness. I know situations look different when a person is surrounded by uncertainty, but I am convinced I never would have learned the significance of hearing the voice of God while in unfamiliar places had I not been in the worship service that day.

A worship service is a varied experience and most of us look forward to praising God, singing, and praying. Because of my experience with a life threatening health issue, I now look to worship for wellness. It serves my wellness to be in the worship service. It serves my health to gather with others in the presence of God. I feel better and more spiritually grounded on the healthy side of the experience. But I needed the service on the ill side as well.

When a disease such as cancer enters a person's life, there is a sense of urgency about life and good health. We try to find the right balance. Somewhere in the midst the worship leads us to understand that the quality and quantity of life is a gift of God, and that what you make of it is what has the potential to please God. And when this realization is shared, it strengthens the body of believers that gather to worship in God's loving care.

A Womanist Perspective on Spiritual Practices

LINDA H. HOLLIES

When people say "black Church," three powerful words immediately come to mind: women, music and preaching. "In the beginning" God ordained Mother Eve to carry "The Church" within her womb and bring him forth to eliminate the conniving, deceitful devil! The Garden of Eden was in Africa, a fact we often fail to remember. Its inhabitants were dark skinned people who multiplied and moved into the rest of the world. All Biblical people were people of color. Eve was a woman of color. And, when her "child," Jesus, arose from the dead, generations later, it was another woman of color, Mary Magdalene, who met him and was given the mandate to go and tell the disciples that resurrection had occurred!

Women make up the majority of the black church. Women sing in the choirs, compose music, and direct choirs. And, women lead the majority of the black church's teaching ministry, Christian education, and spiritual formation. God called Sarah to be mother of the Jewish nation; her servant Hagar also was a vessel as mother of Islam. When Sarah and Abraham sent Hagar away, Hagar received the same inheritance message–that her son would father a nation–as Abraham did. God spoke to her. God has never had a problem with using women.

Jephthah's daughter called the very first women's conference women, according to Judges 11. Each year, the Order of The Eastern Star lifts up her example as the epitome of faithfulness to God. This young woman's father sacrificed the "first thing" that came out of his home as a "deal" with God for winning a victory for his tribe. However, it was his only child who came to greet him and she only asked for three months away, with her sister-friends, before she willingly submitted to being sacrificed. This young woman of color inspired Nannie Helen Burrough to create in 1906 what we now know as National Women's Day in the National Baptist Church. Anglo churches do not celebrate these annual days. But, to uplift the work, worth, and ministry of women, Mrs. Burrough wrote:

> A million women praying? A million women singing? A million women desiring? . . . it would mean spiritual dynamite that would blast Satan's greatest stronghold and drive sin to it's native health . . . we are in desperate need of women learning to become public speakers, and dedicated to a definite cause for which to speak . . .[1]

In the New Testament, Lydia, an astute businesswoman, became a partner for good news with the Apostle Paul. When Paul arrived in Macedonia–according to Acts 16:11-15–Lydia listen to him, believed the gospel, and then offered to take the apostle into her home. She assisted in spreading the church among gentiles. Paul was not ashamed to list her attributes and contributions. In addition, Paul greeted many other notable women in his thanksgivings in Roman 16. The extended missionary work and in-depth compassion that led to what we now know as deaconess and nuns may be traced to the ministry of women in the early church.

The new church at Philippi had several notable women of color in leadership. Paul writes in Philippians 4: 2: "I plead with Euodia and I plead with Syntyche to agree with each other in the Lord." This text alludes to conflict between the two women. Likewise, relationship issues among women plague congregations today.

Noting the struggle for women in ordained ministry, Cheryl Gilkes Townsend says the picture for women is "not good." While other male-dominated professions, like law and medicine, have affirmed women's leadership, electing women to high offices in professional guilds, "church with the great mass appeal in black communities facing the greatest crisis have thrown up the greatest barriers to women's empowerment in their national bodies and local congregations."[2] Women's ordination is still very restrictive in some black church organizations, even though historically women have led ministry through Sunday schools, vacation Bible schools, and mission departments. Additionally, women raise monies for historical black colleges. Women have led choirs and sang and composed songs that reflect the black church's theology. To speak of "good music" requires that we talk about contributions black women make through compositions.

In her book, *God Don't Like Ugly,* homiletics professor, Teresa L. Fry Brown provides much insight into the way women of color led through song. Fry Brown uncovers several subtle and quiet ways women of color have always led within the black church. She says black women often "preached" prolifically using song, including such women as Clara Ward, Lucie Campbell, Mahalia Jackson, Aretha Franklin, Sandra Crouch, and Sweet Honey and The Rock. Because gospel music is biblically based, lyrics are not tied to one particular time period, subject, age, gender, denomination, or racial ethnic group. For example, in 1970, Margaret Douroux wrote *Give Me A Clean Heart.* Based on Psalm 51:10, the song is a prayer that relates the power of God to transform our minds and emotions to make us amenable to God and not to the praises of humanity. Douroux's song exemplifies the way music provides a critical opportunity to teach or to share community values and beliefs. Women and youth make up most choirs in black churches, as they "rehearse and remember" the theology, spirituality, and beliefs of their denominations primarily under the direction of women musicians and teachers.[3]

Not only have women led the church in music, women also have embraced the church's preaching ministry. Women have started entire denominations, built churches and kept the doors open until a male "preacher-pastor" could come along and take lead. In her book, *Sisters in The Wilderness: The Challenge of Womanist God-Talk, (*Orbis Books, 1993) Dr. Delores Williams provides us with an account of many women who have walked the desert journey of Hagar and birthed churches in their wilderness experiences. The role call of women who led include women like Ida Wells Barnett, a noted leader in the anti-lynching movement; Mary McLeod Bethune, a graduate of Moody Bible Institute and street preacher, who founded what is now Bethune Cookman College and served the nation under the presidency of Franklin D. Roosevelt; Mary Church Terrill, women's clubs founder; Harriet Tubman, slave deliverer; Sojourner Truth and Maria Stewart, great anti-slavery preachers; and Rosa Parks, civil rights movement activist. Each woman of color's leadership inspired others and had a powerful impact on the world. Each woman used her own unique style to make a permanent, positive impact upon our lives! They were pastors without titles, ordination, or permission!

Open Wide the Freedom Gates![4]–about women's leadership in the black church–is a must-read book. Written by Dorothy Height, one of the nation's matriarchs, the book is a memoir that tells her story as a young woman called to ordained ministry. Height tried to enroll in New York Seminary in 1924, but was denied. Graduating from the college across the street, she went to work of the YWCA and learned all they could teach her administratively. Later, she took over leadership for The National Council of Negro Women, at the behest of Mary McLeod Bethune. She was "pastor" of this august group for forty-one years, with her primary mantra as "civil and women's rights"!

Though she was denied the right to enter seminary, Height's presence at Susan Johnson-Cook's installation reflected a growing change in attitudes toward women's leadership in black churches. Johnson-Cook was installed as "pastor" of the largest, continuous interdenominational gathering of black pastors, the Hampton Minister's Conference, held yearly at Hampton University in Virginia. Height gave her testimony and passed her leadership mantle to Johnson-Cook. The service was a high moment where no male leader presided! Without "official" permission, Height, Coretta Scott King, and presidential candidate and former Senator Carol Mosely Braun all gathered at the installation and signified that women continue to lead the black church without apology!

The black church has a great legacy of strong women who have persevered despite sexism that continues to prevail. black women have never faltered in their determination to serve God, uplift their nation, and to lift others as they climb! Black women are faithful and faith-filled, trusting God as they continue to minister. Whether as laywomen, women working outside the home, stay-at-home moms, or retired women, there are always those nurturing women who are steadfast, unmovable and always abounding within the black church's center. As they age, church mothers pass along the wisdom of the ages that make the black church such a powerful symbol of God, alive and well in the world.

The above named women have left us their testimony as to how their light shined. They passed the torch to each of us. What will we contribute so that our daughters might read our records in the annals of history in the years to come? I believe women can offer these instructions: Focus on God. Give service in the name of Jesus Christ. Allow your gifts to be used by the power of the Holy Spirit and make a permanent, positive impact where you are located today! May it be so now and forever, for it is the divine will of The Ancient of Days!

Notes

[1] Excerpted from Nannie Helen Burrough's pamphlet: Who Started Women's Day, in Cheryl Townsend Gilkes: *If It Wasn't For The Women* (Maryknoll, NY: Orbis Books, 2001), 114.
[2] Gilkes, *If It Wasn't for the Women,* 210.
[3] Teresa Fry Brown, *God Don't Like Ugly: African American Women Handing On Spiritual Values* (Nashville, TN: Abingdon, 2000) 90-91.
[4] Dorothy Height, *Open Wide the Freedom Gates: A Memoir,* Copyright 2003, Dorothy Height, published by PublicAffairs a member of the Perseus Books Group.